Through the Valley

Bill and Jan
may you know God's
presence and power to
provide for your need

Blessings

Jeff

Through the Valley

Biblical-Theological Reflections on Suffering

JEFF WISDOM

WITH EXCERPTS FROM CHRIS WISDOM'S JOURNAL

WIPF & STOCK · Eugene, Oregon

THROUGH THE VALLEY
Biblical-Theological Reflections on Suffering

Wipf & Stock
An Imprint of Wipf and Stock Publishers
199 W. 8th Ave., Suite 3
Eugene, OR 97401
www.wipfandstock.com

ISBN 13: 978-1-61097-390-8
Manufactured in the U.S.A.

To Brian, Meg, Tim, Jeffrey, and Sophia,
our children who bring us great joy;
to Joe, our son-in-law, for whom we give thanks to God;
and to Colton, our grandson, who always makes us smile.

Preface

THE EMOTION OF THE moment was overwhelming. It was an ordinary, everyday experience; my youngest two children—aged nine and ten at the time—were rounding the corner of our home as they played with joyful enthusiasm. In the preceding weeks, the diagnosis of a stage IV cancer had jolted my sense of safety and security. Now this sight consumed me emotionally because I realized that I could no longer take such experiences for granted. I, indeed, could not count on being here tomorrow. I would have professed this as a belief for most of my life, but now I was overwhelmed with the notion that I might not be here for very much longer to see and to enjoy life with my family. The emotion flooded over me, and I wept as I mourned even the idea of this loss.

I very much wish that I had not written this book. More particularly, I wish that I had never experienced the scourge of cancer. But God has graciously brought me through a time of trouble that I could not have anticipated. I would like to say that I no longer take life for granted, but I freely admit that I have slipped back into the comfortable life that I had led prior to my diagnosis. In some ways I will never be the same, but in some equally important ways I have forgotten the urgency of that horrible experience. I have allowed myself to be deceived into believing and behaving as if I will really be here forever after all, even though I know this is not really true.

In the opening scene of M. Night Shyamalan's *The Village*, a father sits beside his young child's casket and the open grave into which this father's son will soon be buried.[1] This grieving father, who lives in a society that has attempted to flee from the suffering and pain of this world, later poignantly says that we can run from trouble, but trouble will find us out. Most who read this will have experienced the truth that trouble, pain, and hardship in life find us—some much more traumatic than my

1. Shyamalan, *The Village*.

ix

own. Some will be in the midst of trouble now. For some who read this neither will have been true, but indeed, sooner or later, trouble in this life will find us all.

This book is an attempt to sort out some biblical-theological reflections on suffering. It is biblical-theological in that its goal is to reflect on God's promises, which are the divine power given to us to provide us with all that we need for life and godliness (2 Pet 1:3–4). It is reflective in that it does not address the topic of suffering generally, but is instead the very personal reflection on Scripture and my own experience during and after a time of suffering for me and also for my family. This book's scope thus is limited because it is an attempt at a biblical theology of suffering that is refracted through a particular time of trouble for me. This is not a research project on the topic of suffering, but rather the very personal and biblical-theological reflection on my own experience with cancer. Thus the books and commentaries cited in this book are selective, and these sources are suggestive of some of the literature that has impacted my own thinking on the various topics and that I recommend for further reflection and study. I especially commend the works on biblical theology by T. Desmond Alexander[2] and Scott Hafemann.[3]

This experience of the struggle with cancer is sufficiently common that it is hoped that these reflections may be helpful. This book also does not attempt to be an exhaustive study of the topic of suffering, but rather it attempts to touch upon some important Scripture on this topic. The heart of this book is the description of how God's promises in Scripture sustained me through a very deep and dark valley and how I learned to trust him even—and especially—in the midst of unanswered and unresolved questions. Additionally, excerpts from a journal that my wife kept during this battle with cancer complement the topic for each chapter as we walked together through this valley. We selected these excerpts together, and their inclusion in this book provides a glimpse into her perspective on this experience from diagnosis through treatment to remission. These excerpts are placed at the beginning and the end of each chapter. I did not read Chris's journal until after I completed the draft for this book, and these excerpts are intended to provide a brutally honest perspective on walking with a loved one through a very dark valley of

2. Alexander, *From Eden to New Jerusalem*.

3. Hafemann, *The God of Promise and the Life of Faith*.

suffering. This book is my biblical-theological reflection on suffering; her journal entries are the response and reflection in the midst of suffering.

I have served two churches in Massachusetts as a pastor, and I am now an instructor at a Christian College in rural northern Minnesota and a part-time pastor of a small country church. After my first year of teaching at this college, I was diagnosed with a very advanced cancer, one that had already spread to my bone marrow. I have always firmly believed that the Bible teaches that God is sovereign over all of life, but I must confess that the timing of all this left me more than a little confused. Frankly, it made absolutely no sense to me for God to call me to move my family away from relationships cultivated over a decade and a half. It also made very little sense to me for God to move me away from some very fine medical facilities in New England to a rural and remote part of northern Minnesota. Almost nothing about this made much sense to me.

I tell my students that, in my view, one of the greatest needs for the church today is a biblical-theology of suffering. This book is not actually intended to meet this massively important need, but rather I hope it may make a contribution to a part of this important topic for Christians today. It is not intended to address every aspect of the topic of suffering, but rather to reflect biblically on the kind of suffering that comes as the result of the unexpected disease of cancer which ravaged through my life and through my family.[4] Suffering and pain in this life are the result of a variety of factors, including poor choices we make and poor choices that others make. The topic of this book instead is the suffering and pain that come as a result of living in a fallen world, especially the suffering that comes through disease and death.

This book has three parts. The first section makes some biblical-theological reflections on the topic of suffering, especially on the importance of God's presence through suffering, the problem of suffering, and God's plan to address and to remedy this problem. This is not at all meant to be an exhaustive discussion of this important topic, but rather it hits some of the high points of what Scripture says about the

4. There are a number of books that address the problem of evil more broadly and the place of suffering within this theological problem. See for example, Carson, *How Long, O Lord?*; Wright, *Evil and the Justice of God*; Boyd, *Is God to Blame?*; Hauerwas, *Naming the Silences*; and Spencer and Spencer, *Joy through the Night*. These authors approach this topic from a variety of theological perspectives.

suffering of God's people as they live in this fallen world. In particular, the contribution of the Psalms and the Apostle Paul are central to these biblical-theological reflections. Others parts of Scripture could and should be included in a more comprehensive biblical-theological study. These are not biblical-theological reflections in the abstract, but ones refracted through my own recent experience of suffering during a battle with cancer. In the second section, some of the lessons learned during this time of suffering are explored. The experience of God's grace met us in some powerful and surprising ways in this time of suffering. These lessons were not necessarily learned for the first time during this period of my life, but they grew deeper roots into my life. And I continue to grow in these areas. In the third section, I confess and explore some of the struggle during this time of trouble. I do not claim to have mastered everything with which I struggled. I would like to say that I know the reason for this time of suffering, but I don't. I can see some of the ways God has used this in my life, but certainly there is much more that remains hidden to me, and perhaps always will remain hidden. Most of this has been a surprise to me, but in hindsight I can see how the seeds for this had been dormant in my life for many years only to sprout and grow vigorously when I was ill. I continue to wrestle with some of these issues to this day.

Acknowledgments

I HAVE LEARNED SO much from so many people, but I want especially to thank Dr. Scott Hafemann and Prof. James D. G. Dunn for all they have taught me about biblical theology. I have grown so much in my understanding of the story of redemption in Scripture from their tutelage. My perspective on Scripture's teaching has benefited richly through their impact on my thinking about this difficult topic. I am grateful to Dawn Buzay, whose careful proofreading has improved this book at many points. She cheerfully offered her expertise, and I am thankful for this. I want to thank Todd MacDonald for his generosity in allowing me to use his lyrics in my book. His songs have encouraged me very much in my walk of faith, especially when I was ill. He is a dear brother in Christ, who himself is walking through a very dark valley. I am especially grateful to my wife, Chris, with whom I have shared life for thirty years now. She has loved me when I have not always been so loveable, and she has been my partner in all of life. This is especially true with the writing of this book. She has read each chapter with care and has offered many helpful responses. Excerpts from her journal that she kept during my illness are included with each chapter to provide a spouse's view of the struggle with cancer. My reflections in this book look back from the vantage point of five years; her reflections are those from within this horrid experience. We have generally left these excerpts without much or any editing. Even some fragments are left untouched to give a sense of the bluntness of this experience for her. I am most of all thankful to God for how he sustained me through this valley. God's presence and promise were, are, and, by God's grace, will be my hope in life.

Soli Deo gloria.

PART ONE

Biblical-Theological Reflections on Suffering

1

God's Promise

Even though I walk through the valley of the shadow of death, I will fear no evil, for you are with me; your rod and your staff they comfort me.

—PSALM 23:4

July 31, 2005

Here begins a new chapter in our lives. The future just ahead seems a bit frightening. There are so many unanswered questions at this point, and some of the questions may never be answered.

Holding fast to God and his promises is about to be tested. All we have learned so far in our Christian walk as individuals and together has come to meet us at a crucial point. Will our faith endure?

On July 20th at a surgical consultation, the first words of the possibility of cancer became real. On July 22nd Jeff had surgery to remove two very large lymph nodes from his left armpit. That day, it became more real that cancer was a definite possibility. We were told we would have the pathology report by July 28th. The surgeon wanted a second opinion on the nodes that were removed and sent the biopsy down to the Mayo Clinic.

But again at the July 28th appointment, there was more talk of cancer and chemotherapy. The type . . . lymphoma. I have no idea how to spell these "cancer" words, but I'm about to learn a whole new list of vocabulary words.

Monday, August 1st Jeff will undergo a C.T. scan of his chest, abdomen and pelvis. I wonder why not his neck since there are lymph nodes there also. The next day we meet with the oncologist—I suppose to hear the Mayo Clinic's report and the C.T. report. Oh! And of course to discuss when and what kind of chemotherapy he will have to receive, which I believe is to begin about one month after surgery.

I wonder how this will affect Jeff? How sick will it make him? How will it interrupt his job and mine if I need to care for him? Will he let me help? Or will he pretend to be strong and go through this alone, while I (and the kids) watch? And how will all this affect the children?

It is one of the things about pastoral ministry that I miss the most. It is not a very pleasant or enjoyable time, but it is a profoundly significant time in the lives of families. I miss the privilege granted to me as pastor to be with families in times of crisis and grief. Certainly I do not miss the pain and grief itself, and I very much wish that no one ever had to endure this. But we live in a fallen world, and suffering, grief, and pain do indeed find us. I miss the opportunity to be with people when they are walking through some of the deepest valleys of life.

This admission surprises me. When I was in seminary and was anticipating the ministry, even the notion of pastoral care during times of crisis scared me to death! I could never imagine myself as adequate for this task. I am not sure if I ever reached the place where I felt adequate, and I am glad for this because I never felt complacency during these times of pastoral care. I never was very sure of what to say or what to do, except to be with families in the hospital or in the home. I would pray with them and simply read Scripture. Sometimes I merely sat in silence with them.

When I first began to sit with families to plan a funeral service, I regularly asked if they had a passage of Scripture they wanted to include in the service. Without exception, the first passage mentioned was Psalm 23. It really did not seem to matter much, or at all really, whether those who had lost a loved one were long-time members of the church or had little or no connection to a church family. After a while, I began simply to assume Psalm 23 and to ask if there were any other passages from Scripture that the family might suggest for the funeral service. For whatever reason, the familiar language of "The LORD is my shepherd; I shall not want" speaks to us in the midst of pain and grief. Whatever the spiritual place of the people whom I served during the time of the loss of a loved one, Psalm 23 was a well known and beloved place in Scripture to turn for comfort.

Psalm 23 is a comfort to God's people because it affirms the promise of God's presence with them as their shepherd: "The LORD is my shepherd; I shall not want" (Ps 23:1a). The image of shepherd in the time of this psalm implied a high level of bravery, strength, and authority for the one who cared for the sheep. Shepherds needed to be brave and to have strength because they needed to protect the flock from vicious predators. The shepherd was one who protected the sheep. Thus the cultural world of the Old Testament regularly associated the king with the image of a shepherd because a primary role for the king was to protect his people from danger and enemies.[1] This statement in Psalm 23 that the Lord is shepherd is an affirmation of the Lord's sovereign strength. It is a reference to his role as protector. Thus the shepherd was one who was both willing and able to protect the sheep from danger. Sheep also cannot provide for themselves, and the shepherd must provide everything for them. As Lawson notes, "Left to themselves, sheep lack everything, being totally helpless and defenseless animals who cannot care for themselves. But under the shepherd's care, all their needs are abundantly met."[2] As shepherd for his people, God provides for their needs and protects them from danger, even when they walk through the valley of the shadow of death.

This psalm is saturated with statements of what God does as a shepherd for the flock over which he exercises his sovereign care.

> He makes me lie down in green pastures.
> He leads me beside still waters.
> He restores my soul.
> He leads me in paths of righteousness
> for his name's sake.
> Even though I walk through the valley of the shadow of death,
> I will fear no evil,
> for you are with me;
> your rod and your staff
> they comfort me. (Ps 23:1b–4)

The Lord is a good shepherd and provides what his sheep need, even when they are faced with the specter of death. The Lord is the one who tends to the needs of his sheep. He guides the sheep to safe and secure pasture in which they are able to lie down. He leads them to places where their basic need for water is met. Both of these needs are pressing concerns for sheep in the desert or semi-desert environment of the Ancient Near East, and the specific references to the Lord's provision

1. Goldingay, *Psalms,* 1:348; and Wilson, *Psalms,* 1:431–32.
2. Lawson, *Psalms 1–75,* 432.

where the sheep may "lie down in green pastures" and "still waters" both imply a place of rest and security.[3] The Lord, as shepherd, provides the place for the sheep to find their need for nourishment and restoration met in his gracious provision.

Psalm 23 then shifts its attention from a place of restful stillness near God's place of provision to his guidance and protection as the sheep move from place to place. The Lord provides direction toward righteousness for the praise of his glory; he directs them on the right paths for their welfare so that his glory as good shepherd is reflected in his provision for them. Perhaps most importantly, it is the promise of God's presence through the valley of the shadow of death that is the basis for confidence and comfort: "Even though I walk through the valley of the shadow of death, I will fear no evil, for you are with me; your rod and your staff they comfort me" (Ps 23:4). His shepherd's rod protects from danger that they may encounter, and his shepherd's staff guides the sheep along the way. Both remind of God's presence.

> So the shepherd's presence makes itself felt by means of rod and staff. . . . The shepherd would carry [a rod] attached to his belt as the weapon with which to attack animals and thus protect the sheep. His staff is the cane on which he might lean for support, though it is also the means by which a shepherd might keep the sheep in order and knock down olives for them to eat. The two objects thus "comfort" the sheep in different ways.[4]

Despite the fearsome nature of some experiences in life, there is no fear of ultimate harm because the Lord is present with his people. Psalm 23 moves from the place of restful contentment in the place of God's provision (Ps 23:2–3a), through a journey along a pathway on which he is leading and protecting (Ps 23:3b), to the place of a fearsome and terrifying threat to life itself (Ps 23:4). This psalm affirms the Lord's presence in these vastly different experiences in life.

Perhaps this movement in Psalm 23 from the tranquil to the troubled is intended to remind us that we need to trust in God in each and every circumstance in life. The natural tendency for most is to turn to God in trust during times of crisis. But Psalm 23, along with much of the rest of Scripture, reminds us that we are creatures who depend on our creator in all of life. Whether the experience is one of tranquil rest in

3. Ibid., 349–50.
4. Ibid., 351.

Prepare in the tranquil times

green pastures and beside still waters or it is one of the deeply troubling valleys of the shadow of death, the Lord is the shepherd who is present, protects, and provides. And the movement in Psalm 23 from the tranquil to the troubled may be an implicit encouragement to deepen one's trust in God during more peaceful times so that when the storms of life come this faith may sustain through the strongest of gale-force winds. [5]

When I was nine years old, our family lived in Gulfport, Mississippi. In August of that year, Hurricane Camille roared through the gulf coast and left a swath of devastation in its wake. I remember well the preparations many took to get ready for this storm, the intensity of the winds that night (it sounded like a freight train was rumbling just outside all night long), and the complete and utter destruction of that category-five storm, especially along the gulf coastline. For several days in advance of the arrival of this massive storm, businesses and homeowners all along the gulf coast of Mississippi, Alabama, and Louisiana anxiously and expectantly made preparations for its arrival. Property and possessions were secured as much as possible. Many who lived along the coastline evacuated to safer locations farther inland.

The experience of a hurricane is devastating, indeed. When a hurricane is imminent, many people make preparations before it strikes: windows are boarded with plywood, boats are removed from the water or are moved out to sea, and outdoor furniture is stored indoors. All of these are steps taken in order to ride out the storm. Often the media will report on these preparations for several days in advance of a big storm. The best time to prepare for a major storm is, quite obviously, before it begins. How foolish it would be to begin to prepare for such a severe storm after it has begun! In a similar way, the best time to strengthen trust in God is before a major storm strikes. Such growth in trust during peaceful times helps to anchor our heart and our mind before major catastrophe strikes. Once a major time of trouble comes, it may be too late. Perhaps the movement from the tranquil to the troubled in Psalm 23 is an implicit encouragement to recognize and respond to this need for preparation.

The phrase "the valley of the shadow of death" used here suggests any deep, narrow, and dangerous valley through which the sheep must pass.[6] It is a place where fear and danger stalk every step. This is the typi-

---

5. Carson, *How Long, O Lord?*

6. Goldingay, *Psalms*, 1:351; and Wilson, *Psalms*, 434.

cal experience when passing through such a valley (referred to in that part of the world as a *wadi*) even today. Wilson describes a walk through such a valley:

> I remember hiking down Wadi Qelt from Jerusalem to Jericho with a friend. A narrow, ancient Roman aqueduct, still flowing with water, clung to the canyon wall at a height of several hundred feet. We began our journey following the rugged footpath on the opposite canyon wall, dipping at points to the bottom of the wadi and back up the other side. It took only about two such trips down into the shadowy depths of the stifling heat at the wadi bottom (and this was in the early morning!) and scrambling back up the steep limestone wall to regain the path, before we overcame our natural reluctance of heights and continued our journey walking along the outer rim of the aqueduct—or, in the most narrow portions, in the aqueduct itself.
>
> Even so my two-liter bottle of water was depleted halfway through our journey. When we stopped at St. George's monastery to replenish our supply, the water tap in the courtyard first emitted only steam, and then a grudging stream of almost boiling water. I had enough trouble dragging myself up and down those rocky hills. I cannot imagine the difficulty of herding a whole flock of sheep through the "valley of the shadow of death."[7]

The time spent in the valley of the shadow of death is actually assumed in Psalm 23, but even this does not call into question the Lord as the good shepherd for his people because he is with them, and he is their shepherd in any experience in life. For even in the experience of this fearsome valley, the Lord is present with his sheep.

The second half of Psalm 23 moves from the image of the Lord as good shepherd to the image of the Lord as gracious host.[8] He provides for his people all of the things that a gracious host provides for guests invited into his home: "You prepare a table before me in the presence of my enemies; you anoint my head with oil; my cup overflows. Surely goodness and mercy shall follow me all the days of my life, and I shall dwell in the house of the Lord forever" (Ps 23:5–6). The Lord prepares and places food on the table, he provides the cup that overflows, and he anoints with the oil provided to restore the guest in his home.[9] These

---

7. Wilson, *Psalms*, 434.

8. Goldingay, *Psalms*, 1:346; and Wilson, *Psalms*, 436.

9. Goldingay, *Psalms*, 1:352.

describe a gracious host who provides for those invited into his home. Yet even this gracious provision is in the very presence of enemies, in the very presence of danger.[10] As a good shepherd, God is present with his sheep, and he provides for them in the midst of danger. As Psalm 23 concludes, it affirms that God's goodness and mercy are in relentless pursuit of God's people: "Surely goodness and mercy shall follow me all the days of my life, and I shall dwell in the house of the Lord forever" (Ps 23:6). This appropriate conclusion to this psalm affirms that God's goodness and mercy are constant companions and that the psalmist will always dwell in God's presence.

Psalm 23 affirms that the Lord provides and protects because he is present in all of life. He is a good shepherd who provides for his sheep and protects them from predators. He is a gracious host who provides for his guests, and they are always in his presence. The constant presence of God that is assumed in the first half of Psalm 23 is explicitly emphasized in the final two verses; God is present "all the days of my life" and "forever." He is present with them even when they are walking through the valley of the shadow of death. It is a precious promise: that God, the good shepherd, is with us in all of life, even when we are facing pain, grief and suffering. This promise has grown increasingly precious to me. But I have to confess that I often did not sense God's presence with me in the darkest moments of my treatment for cancer. God often felt absent, indifferent, and uncaring.[11]

I learned that cancer is a lonely experience. I felt very much alone. This may seem to be an odd thing to say because in many ways I had never been the focus of so much attention from people in my entire life. I have probably not received as many cards and notes of encouragement throughout my lifetime as I did during that year. Many people who lived all over the world were praying for me. Many friends and family were very generous with financial gifts. My family was a constant encouragement to me. My wife was supportive and encouraging in ways that I can only begin to acknowledge publicly. She lovingly and graciously did things for me that no person should ever be asked to do. I was loved throughout this year in many, many ways. Yet when a person is forced

---

10. Wilson, *Psalms*, 436.

11. On the important but neglected theme in Scripture of God's apparent absence, see Terrien, *The Elusive Presence*.

to stare into the face of his or her own mortality, this is something done alone. I have never felt so alone in my entire life.

I did not always feel that God was with me during my illness. There were many days when the pain caused by the cancer and the chemotherapy seemed overwhelming. I experienced pain in parts of my body that had never known pain before. On several occasions, I had pain and weakness in my hips that caused them to feel as though they buckled and came out of joint, and I collapsed to the floor. Often I felt alone, even when there were others in our home. Many times I wanted to give up and give in to this disease. The struggle seemed overwhelming because it often seemed as though I bore its weight alone. I continued to pray and to cry out to God, but this rarely changed my physical situation at that moment. Actually, it never changed my circumstances on any given day. I felt very much alone in a world that quite literally was trying to consume me. Cancer is, of course, a disease that attempts to consume in order to grow and survive. Yet as it grows and spreads, it kills the body that it is consuming. And quite honestly, when something is attempting to consume us, the most natural and normal response is fear.

In the face of the prospect of death, fear is a natural response. Although fear is real and is not to be denied, it cannot overwhelm the one who trusts in the shepherd's rod and staff to comfort. The mere mention of comfort as a need met in this psalm implies the reality that fear is sometimes the experience of God's people. Psalm 23 implies that the answer for fear is not to deny its existence, but rather to turn to the protection and provision of the shepherd when fearsome circumstances in life assault us. When fear grips our heart and our soul, Scripture teaches us to trust in God, who is the good shepherd. As I was writing these words, a friend posted this Scripture online, and it encouraged me anew: "When I am afraid, I will trust in you. In God, whose word I praise, in God I trust; I shall not be afraid. What can flesh do to me?" (Ps 56:3–4). The digital age in which we live provides pleasantly new opportunities for the encouragement of one another! When fear grips our heart and our soul, this psalm teaches us to trust in God. No matter what we face in life, trust in God, our creator, sustainer, and sovereign Lord.

Another psalm of David affirms the Lord's presence and provision in the face of fear. This psalm expresses trust in God despite circumstances: "The LORD is my light and my salvation; whom shall I fear? The LORD is the stronghold of my life; of whom shall I be afraid?" (Ps 27:1).

This psalm describes the danger of opponents and the harm they intend to inflict (Ps 27:2–3). These opponents intend to "eat up my flesh" (v. 2), and they are an enemy encamped as a besieging army intent on destruction (v. 3). These are two different images for times of extreme terror. This psalm, however, affirms that the Lord is the one who delivers and the one who is a refuge in such a time of trouble. Yet the danger and its accompanying fear is real. Goldingay helps us to see this more clearly; he writes, "The declaration that Yhwh is my light is characteristically spelled out as implying that Yhwh is deliverer. That being so, I have no reason to fear. Yet stating this somehow draws attention to the fact that evidently I do have reason for fear."[12] Fear is the natural response to terrifying experiences. In the midst of terrifying times of trouble, Psalm 27 calls for a present and abiding trust in the Lord.[13]

This ongoing trust in the Lord despite the experience of suffering compels the psalmist to petition the Lord to respond to this need (Ps 27:7–12). Psalm 27 recalls the Lord's past deliverance as a foundation for the present petition in the midst of trouble. Trust in the Lord in the present, despite circumstances, is not merely wishful thinking; instead, trust in the Lord is grounded on his past action and activity on behalf of the psalmist. Goldingay describes this connection between God's past provision and presence and the present need expressed in this psalm: "The recollection of pressure, prayer, and divine response paves the way for further prayer under pressure while looking for a further divine response."[14] The psalmist calls aloud to the Lord for him to hear and to answer this petition uttered in pain (v. 7). The Lord's presence is sought because he is the one who is a help and a deliverer (vv. 8–9). Even when parents fail and forsake, the Lord is faithful (v. 10). Parents may typically (but not always) be dependable and reliable, but in a fallen world even they may fail to provide and protect. The Lord is always faithful. The Lord's presence is sought when people have completely abandoned the psalmist.[15] The Lord's faithful guidance and protection is proclaimed (vv. 11–12). This is the experience of trust in the midst of pain and trouble; those who trust turn to the Lord in their experience of pain and call out to him. Trust does not mean that I need to deny the reality of the fear

12. Goldingay, *Psalms*, 1:392.

13. Wilson, *Psalms*, 483.

14. Goldingay, *Psalms*, 1:396.

15 Ibid., 398.

and even the terror that assaults me. Trust means that I turn to the Lord in such fearsome and terrifying circumstances in life. It means that I turn to the faithful one who is my help and my deliverance. It means that I seek the comfort, protection, and provision that are found in the Lord's presence.

Nestled in this psalm of petition to the Lord in a time of need is the affirmation that God is present and will provide.

> One thing have I asked from the LORD,
>   that will I seek after:
> that I may dwell in the house of the LORD
>   all the days of my life,
> to gaze upon the beauty of the LORD
> and to inquire in his temple.
>
> For he will hide me in his shelter
>   in the day of trouble;
> he will conceal me under the cover of his tent;
>   he will lift me high upon a rock.
> And now my head shall be lifted up
>   above my enemies all around me,
> and I will offer in his tent
>   sacrifices with shouts of joy;
> I will sing and make melody to the LORD. (Ps 27:4–6)

The themes of "dwelling" and "sheltering" indicate God's presence and provision for those in need who call out to him. It suggests a whole-hearted commitment to the Lord as the one who is a help and deliverer in the midst of trouble. It is a wholehearted commitment to the Lord, despite present circumstances. As Wilson puts it, "To seek God in this way is not a matter of unfocused searching but a sign of commitment to the way of life he demands and provides. To 'seek' false gods (as in 4:2) is to commit oneself to them. The faithful generation is made up of those who seek the face of Yahweh and commit themselves to him alone."[16] Trust is not a "leap in the dark," but is a dependence upon the God who has worked on our behalf in the past and who has committed himself to work on our behalf in the future.[17]

Psalm 27 concludes with a call—that is, rather, a command—to wait patiently for the Lord to respond (Ps 27:13–14). The fact that these

---

16. Wilson, *Psalms*, 484.

17. Hafemann, *The God of Promise and the Life of Faith*.

are commands indicates that this psalm takes the perspective of perseverance in trust. The implication of these commands to trust is either that one must renew trust in time of trouble or that one must continue to trust in these times. But in either case, the call to trust in the Lord in the context of a psalm that affirms the trustworthiness of the Lord indicates that the previous presence of trust must be maintained.[18] Psalm 27 calls for perseverance in trust. And the person who trusts in God's presence and provision waits upon him to respond and is not consumed with fear.

God's presence with us as we walk through the valley of the shadow of death enables and empowers us to walk faithfully with the God who is present with us even in the midst of suffering. This demonstrates to others that the power to persevere in the Christian life comes from the God who dwells with us. The Apostle Paul emphasized this truth when he wrote to the Corinthians about his own perseverance in and through suffering: "But we have this treasure in jars of clay, to show that the surpassing power belongs to God and not to us" (2 Cor 4:7). Believers, and the fragility of their lives, are compared to jars of clay, which are easily cracked and broken. The image of a jar of clay is one of weakness and suffering.[19] Jars of clay are also intended to contain something else, something that often is of great value. This is exactly what we are—vessels that contain a great treasure. What is this treasure? In this context, it is the Spirit who is transforming believers in Christ into his glorious image (2 Cor 3:12–18) and "the light of the knowledge of the glory of God in the face of Jesus Christ" (2 Cor 4:6). This Christian hope of the glorious presence of God with us gives us a boldness despite suffering (2 Cor 3:12) and enables us not to lose heart in the midst of suffering (2 Cor 4:1).

This treasure is also the new-creation work in believers through which they are being transformed into the image of Christ: "For God, who said, 'Let light shine out of darkness,' has shone in our hearts to give the light of the knowledge of the glory of God in the face of Jesus Christ" (2 Cor 4:6). Paul here refers to God's creative activity in the first chapter of Genesis and compares the new work that God is doing in believers with his creation of the world. God spoke, and light was created. God now creates anew through "the gospel of the glory of Christ, who is the

18. Goldingay, *Psalms*, 1:400.

19. Hafemann, *2 Corinthians*, 182.

image of God" (2 Cor 4:4). Just as God spoke creation into existence in Genesis, so also he is now doing a work of new creation in believers as he shines the light of the knowledge of God's glory in the face of his son, Jesus Christ.[20]

This work of the Spirit who is already in us and the new creation power of God already at work in us—this is the treasure in the jars of clay. God's Spirit is his presence with us, and God's power at work in us gives us the ability to endure life in this fallen world. We are not overwhelmed and overcome by the trouble experienced in a fallen world because God is present with us, and he has provided for us.

> We are afflicted in every way, but not driven to despair; persecuted, but not forsaken; struck down, but not destroyed; always carrying in the body the death of Jesus, so that the life of Jesus may also be manifested in our bodies. For we who live are always being given over to death for Jesus's sake, so that the life of Jesus also may be manifested in our mortal flesh. So death is at work in us, but life in you. (2 Cor 4:8–12)

The trouble is real, and we sometimes feel its full weight bearing down on us. Paul certainly experienced pain and suffering. He described his own experience of suffering as an apostle of Jesus Christ for the sake of Christ and also for the sake of those whom he served in the churches he planted. Paul's endurance of suffering was perhaps more extreme than most (see, for example, 2 Cor 11:23–29). But any and every time believers in Christ endure suffering in a fallen world, it demonstrates the power of the Spirit of God to sustain hope despite suffering and also becomes an opportunity to display the transforming work of God to change us into the very image of Jesus Christ.

> Thus, in drawing out the contemporary significance of Paul's theocentric worldview, we need to keep in focus the ways in which Paul sees the glory of Christ at work among the church. Otherwise, it is simply too easy to become enamored with the false glory of the health and wealth gospel. In our day and age, as in Paul's, the moral transformation into God's character pictured in 3:18 and the endurance in the midst of adversity modeled in 4:1–8 seem too mundane to be miraculous. To consider health more important than holiness, however, is to slight God himself and his work in bringing about the new creation in our midst.

20. Ibid., 175–82.

> For Paul, the reality of the resurrection is already being inaugurated in the conversion of believers into the body of Christ.[21]

God's presence with us empowers our faithful walk with him in this life, even through the pain and suffering of the valley of the shadow of death.

I have learned to trust less in what I feel and more in what God has promised in Scripture. Even when I walked through the valley of the shadow of death, God was with me. When fear stalked my every step, his shepherd's rod and staff comforted me because they reminded me that he was present with me even through these dark days. I learned some very painful lessons on the importance of waiting upon the Lord in the midst of suffering. The weight of this cancer and its treatment often felt overwhelming, but God was with me. This is the promise of Scripture. The question for me was simple and yet profound. Would I give in to the despair or would I trust in what God had promised to me?

> *July 31, 2005*
>
> *Dear God, I'm scared! How will we grow through this new experience or how will we fail? I'm at a loss as to how to pray. I'd like to say "take it all away," but you have allowed this for a reason, unknown to me, maybe to help us become the people you want us to be. So, soften our hearts, soften my heart, so you can mold us! Help me to always seek you and to remember it's not what happens but how I react to what happens that counts. Amen.*

---

21. Ibid., 195–96.

2

The Problem of Pain

My God, my God, why have you forsaken me? Why are you so far from saving me, from the words of my groaning? O my God, I cry by day, but you do not answer, and by night, but I find no rest.

—Psalm 22:1–2

August 2, 2005

Saturday was a bad, ugly morning for me. Fear won, and I gave in. There was some self-pity involved but mainly that was caused by letting the fear seep in, like smoke under a door. It just kept coming. I couldn't stop it. "Forgive me, Lord. I'm sorry!"

Today, the day before our son Tim's 14th birthday, we have a diagnosis. My husband has Hodgkin's Lymphoma—cancer. There are two kinds of Hodgkin's cancer and this is the lesser of the two evils. It's treatable at stages one, two and three. Stage four is also treatable to some degree. We had our consultation with the oncologist, and he gave us the news. Yesterday's C.T. scan did show more enlarged lymph nodes under his left arm and maybe some in the groin area. Blood work also indicated the possibility of prostate cancer so a biopsy is needed.

So now the next step is "staging." That will determine at what stage the cancer is in. After that, he begins the appropriate treatment. There are two more tests (at this point) to help with the staging. On Friday, Jeff will undergo a bone marrow biopsy in the oncologist's office. On Saturday, Jeff leaves for the greatly anticipated baseball trip with his brothers and Dad. He arrives home Friday, and we think the second test will happen on Monday. This test is called a P.E.T. scan, which is a more definitive C.T. scan. But Friday's test will give us a good idea how far along this "thief" is in Jeff's body.

I sat in the doctor's office that Friday afternoon in shock. I heard the words the doctor spoke to me about the results of the most recent medical tests, which included the results of a bone marrow biopsy. But it was very difficult for me to accept them. Prior to this moment when I was assaulted with the worst news possible, I had thought that the most traumatic part of the process of diagnosis and staging of this cancer had been this bone marrow biopsy. Most of the medical tests I had recently undergone were fairly painless, but the bone marrow biopsy was not. When the nurse described the procedure to me as she prepared me for it, I asked her about the level of pain to expect because this biopsy had a reputation—a reputation for pain. She informed me that most patients had told her afterwards that it was not as bad as they had expected. Since I am a fairly trusting person by nature, I relaxed. It may not be so bad, after all.

This was my first mistake. My second mistake was that I remembered this conversation with this nurse and approached the procedure with a very casual posture. I did have enough sense not to look at the size of the needle that the oncologist was to insert into my hipbone. I have a general policy about this; I don't especially care to know the size of a needle that is to be inserted into me! The biopsy was to be bilateral, which meant that bone marrow and bone fragments would be taken from both hipbones. A local anesthetic numbed the flesh and the bone, but the doctor told me that the bone marrow itself would not be numbed. To this day, I am not sure whether it is not possible or simply not preferable for the bone marrow to be affected by the anesthetic.

In either case, the procedure began well. I simply felt pressure as the needle was inserted. Then bone fragments were chipped and gathered through the needle, and this still remained fairly painless. Then there was a gentle "punch" as the needle pushed through the bone. I thought so far, so good. Then the pain began. To his credit, the doctor paused and told me to get ready, and he waited for me to affirm that I was set. He knew to do this because he had previously told me that he had volunteered for this procedure. He had a bone marrow biopsy to provide his own healthy bone marrow for a study while he was in medical school. *He volunteered for this procedure.* I grew to respect his courage very much!

The actual extraction of the bone marrow was very quick—it only seemed to take a few seconds. Yet the sensation of the thin strand of bone marrow as it was extracted was extraordinarily painful for those few seconds. I could feel the narrow strand of bone marrow as the biopsy collected this sample, and the sensation of pain actually began in the back of my calf and seemed to be "pulled along" up the back of my leg. I have called this sensation the "string of pain," and it remains the most unusual sensation of pain that I have ever experienced. It knocked the wind out of me; I felt like I had been sucker punched. In part, I know that I was too relaxed. "It's not so bad after all," I had been told. The doctor asked me how I was, and I responded with a grunt and a groan that I needed "some time" before we went to the other hip. He told me that he would be back in about ten minutes to check on me, and during this time I recalled some of the dormant Lamaze techniques my wife and I had learned in birthing classes many years before. I began to control my breathing, I focused on a spot on the wall, and went to a "happy place." Most importantly, I bore down on the hand of one of the nurses when the time came to collect the second sample of my bone marrow. I had been offered a nurse's hand to hold before the first extraction, but I had declined. I did not repeat that mistake! The second part of this procedure went much better.

After this bone marrow biopsy, we waited. The results of a variety of tests over the previous few weeks had resulted in a diagnosis of Hodgkin's Lymphoma, and these recent results were intended to stage the cancer, to determine how far the disease had progressed in my body. Since the enlarged lymph nodes were restricted to my left armpit, my wife and I were hopeful that it was still in the early stages. The oncologist told us that this disease typically began in the lymph nodes in the upper torso or in the neck, and then moved down through the lymphatic system until it eventually reached the bone marrow and major organs. Previous tests indicated that the cancer was restricted to the lymph nodes in my left armpit so we were hopeful. But the biopsy results shattered this hope. The cancer was in my bone marrow, which made it a stage IV cancer— a very advanced one. The treatment for this cancer was chemotherapy every two weeks for six to eight months. Four specific drugs had proven an effective treatment for this disease over the years, but in stage IV the situation was not so clear. The doctor's attempt to reassure me ("we are still hopeful") rang hollow at the time. This chemotherapy was very, very aggressive. It progressively wore me down physically, mentally, emotionally, and spiritually.

The world is not exactly as God intended. Certainly my world was not as I wanted it to be on that Friday afternoon in August. There is much beauty and joy in this life, but there is also much pain and suffering. The relentless question all Christians face at one time or another is how a good God can allow this pain and suffering as part of the world he created. It is the problem of pain. For some Christians, this question drives them to wonder openly if God has manipulated events and has deceived them so that choices they have made in life—choices apparently made in response to God's perceived will for them at the time—led them directly and painfully into extreme circumstances of suffering.[1] For others, this problem of suffering is so severe that it leads them to leave the faith.[2] Although I don't agree with either conclusion (and the first author really does not either), I understand them better now than I would have prior to my illness.

At one time or another, we all face the problem of pain. In his famous book of this title, C. S. Lewis explores this problem of pain.[3] For most of this very influential work, Lewis has in view the pain that comes from God as discipline intended to correct us or the pain and suffering that are the result of living in a human society that has been granted freedom of choice. Rarely does Lewis specifically engage the kind of suffering in view here—the pain and suffering that come to mortal human beings from the ravages of disease and death. Yet Lewis is very clear that human rebellion is responsible for human suffering of every kind.

The Bible asserts that in the beginning God created (Gen 1:1), and it is emphatic that what he created was good (Gen 1:4, 10, 12, 18, 21, and 25). The creation narrative reaches a climax in the affirmation that "God saw everything that he had made; and behold, it was very good" (Gen 1:31). God created humanity in his image and blessed them so that they might be fruitful and multiply and thus have dominion over all of God's good creation.

> So God created man in his own image, in the image of God he created him; male and female he created them. And God blessed them. And God said to them, "Be fruitful and multiply and fill the earth and subdue it and have dominion over the fish of the sea and over the birds of the heavens and over every living thing that moves on the earth." (Gen. 1:27–28)

1. Feinberg, *Deceived by God? A Journey through Suffering*.
2. Ehrman, *God's Problem*.
3. Lewis, *The Problem of Pain*.

Humanity created in God's image represented him as they filled and exercised dominion over creation.[4]

The people God made are created beings, and thus they are not God. Yet at the same time, the creation narrative indicates that humanity occupies a special and unique place within God's good creation.

> the creation of mankind is marked in verse 26 by the usual "And God said . . ." However, the words of God which follow are not the expected impersonal command: "Let there be a man . . . ." Instead, the words are in the first person; they are the personal expression of the will of God: "Let us make man . . . ." The contrast is striking and shows the central importance the narrative attaches to the creation of man and woman. The effect would be the same as if a speaker in the midst of a formal presentation suddenly broke the cadence of his words and began to talk personally to the audience.[5]

This shift in God's command in creation indicates and highlights the unique place and role of humanity in God's creation. As God's unique and special creation, humanity is intended to fill the earth and exercise dominion over it.

This is the divine mandate given to humanity, and it is a mandate supported and sustained by God's gracious provision: "And God said, 'Behold I have given you every plant yielding seed that is on the face of all the earth, and every tree with seed in its fruit. You shall have them for food'" (Gen 1:29). God's good creation was intended to provide everything that people needed. And as they trusted in his provision for them, they continued in the blessed land God provided.[6] Sin and death only came into play in God's creation as a result of human rebellion; sin and death entered God's good creation when humanity submitted to the temptation to mistrust God and the seduction of becoming like God.

> Now the serpent was more crafty than any other beast of the field that the LORD God had made. He said to the woman, "Did God actually say, 'You shall not eat of any tree in the garden?'" And the woman said to the serpent, "We may eat of the fruit of the trees in the garden, but God said, 'You shall not eat of the fruit of the tree that is in the midst of the garden, neither shall you touch it,

4. Hafemann, *The God of Promise and the Life of Faith*, 23–60.

5. Sailhamer, *Genesis Unbound*, 144.

6. Hafemann, *The God of Promise and the Life of Faith*, 23–60.

lest you die."' But the serpent said to the woman, "You will not
surely die. For God knows that when you eat of it your eyes will
be opened, and you will be like God, knowing good and evil."
(Gen 3:1–5)

In rebellion against God and his commandment, Adam and Eve
submitted themselves to part of God's creation when they listened to and
obeyed the serpent rather than their creator. They were intended to have
dominion over all of creation, but instead they rebelled against God and
obeyed the serpent.

The consequence was the curse, which included the entrance of
death into God's good creation (Gen 2:15–16; 3:19). Even some parts
of God's creation that were intended for our welfare were impacted by
pain and suffering. The intensity of labor and delivery and the work of
people in God's creation were both characterized by pain (Gen 3:16–17).
Death, pain, and suffering were not part of God's original, good creation
but only entered into human experience as a result of human rebellion
against God. God's intention in his creation was to provide for humanity through his gracious presence with them, but their rebellion against
their creator changed this place of divine provision and rest. God's ban-
ishment from his presence meant that humanity was "now competing
with each other and against creation in a world that was no longer hos-
pitable. Mankind's enjoyment of God's 'rest' was over . . . to be banished
from God's presence and to be given over to one's own sinful desires
in this life is 'hell on earth.'"[7] God's good creation had been marred by
the presence of sin and death, and these scourges of humanity were the
result of their rebellion against their creator. The problem of pain was
not originally a part of God's creation, but rather it was introduced into
our world through humanity's fall.[8]

After my first round of chemo, the routine blood work before my
second treatment showed that my white blood cell count was very low,
too low for treatment that day. I was devastated. The doctor had stressed
to me the importance of keeping on schedule, and this schedule for
treatment was every two weeks. To learn that my body was not able to
withstand even one session of chemo without becoming depleted left me

7. Ibid., 64–65.

8. Ibid., 61–81; Carson, *How Long, O Lord?* 41–49; Boyd, *Is God to Blame?* 21–40;
and Spencer and Spencer, *Joy through the Night*, 23–33. These authors approach the
topic of suffering from different theological perspectives, but each traces Scripture's
contention that suffering stems from humanity's rebellion in the garden.

wondering if I could endure this treatment at all. Would I have to stop chemotherapy? Would this leave no medical options for me? The doctor informed me that I would receive a mega-dose of Neupogen, a drug intended to stimulate the body's production of white blood cells. I would then need to receive this drug through injections at home for seven consecutive days during a two-week chemo cycle. These shots were to be my constant companion throughout the months of chemotherapy ahead of me. The side effects of these injections included "mild to moderate" bone pain. In my case, it seemed to be more on the "moderate" side, at least!

I received this first injection of Neupogen in the early afternoon, and by the evening meal time, I was beginning to feel the bone pain, especially in my sternum. But I had forgotten the side effect of bone pain, one of a list of possible side effects explained to me earlier. In the chaos and confusion of that day (at least from my perspective), many of the side effects that had been explained to me quite thoroughly had slipped my mind. When I began to experience a sharp and growing pain in my chest, I became concerned. Great, I thought, not only do I have an advanced cancer, but I am also having a heart attack! Within a few minutes I realized what was happening and had another opportunity to use those Lamaze techniques. This rather intense reaction to a drug intended to help my body fight this cancer began a nearly six month endurance of the pain caused by this drug—pain caused by something intended to help me.

We live in a fallen world that is marred by sin, disease, and death. God created a very good world, but humanity's rebellion against the Creator introduced suffering and death into God's good creation. Now even things that are meant for our welfare can be the source of pain; anyone who has been through or has observed the process of the labor and delivery of a child can attest this. The Bible affirms that pain and suffering are not part of God's original intention for his creation, but are the results of humanity's rebellion against him. The problem of the pain we experience in a fallen world is one of our own making.

The collection of psalms in Scripture includes a variety of forms. Some are thanksgiving psalms that worship the Lord and express thanks to him, and some are wisdom psalms that give instruction concerning choices to be made in life. There are several other kinds of psalms in Scripture, but it is the lament psalms that have lately been a great encouragement to me. A lament psalm is an honest, and sometimes painfully explicit, call to the Lord for help in a time of trouble. Within the context of trust in the Lord, a lament psalm expresses disappointment, confusion, and even despair over the trouble that has assaulted the believer. Typically a lament psalm also affirms the confidence that the prayer will be heard, and the Lord will respond. Thus lament psalms are the believer's honest, heartfelt expression of pain and suffering in prayer to the Lord. Sometimes a lament includes the sense that the Lord has abandoned his people: "My God, my God, why have you forsaken me? Why are you so far from saving me, from the words of my groaning? O my God, I cry by day, but you do not answer, and by night, but I find no rest" (Ps 22:1–2).

Jesus himself called out to God with the words of this psalm (Mark 15:34). Thus Scripture does indeed affirm that the problem of pain is one that humanity has made for themselves, but it also affirms that, in the incarnation of Jesus Christ, God himself has entered into our fallen world and has suffered in our place and for our benefit and blessing.[9] God is not detached from our fallen world and our suffering in it. In the incarnation of Jesus Christ and his passion in Gethsemane and on the cross, he took on the pain and suffering that is so basic and fundamental to our fallen world in order to redeem us from it. Jesus's own experience in Gethsemane and on the cross demonstrate clearly the extent that God was willing to go to redeem humanity from this fallen world—the death of God's beloved Son for us, who live in a fallen world that is marred by pain, suffering, and death (Rom 8:31–39).

Psalm 22 thus is the prayer of a person who is in the midst of pain and who is experiencing affliction and abandonment.

> The Psalter presents it as a model for the prayer of ordinary Israelites or Christians when they experience affliction. . . . they may have the sense of being personally overwhelmed, feeling they are falling apart, nearing collapse, staring death in the face. . . . they may be aware that God has abandoned them: God is not intervening to deliver them. . . . God does not answer their prayers. The psalm encourages people to own that this is their experience and not to hide from it. It thus questions the common Christian way of encouraging people to cope with suffering by reassuring them that God is present with them in their suffering. God was not always with this suppliant and does not expect us to pretend that this is so when it is not.[10]

[handwritten margin note: ? / Heb 13.5b]

9. Carson, *How Long, O Lord?* 179–95.

10. Goldingay, *Psalms,* 1:340–41.

Lament psalms thus can include the excruciatingly painful experience of abandonment to misery and even death.

Psalm 22 is a lament psalm that reflects a brutal honesty about the pain and suffering experienced in this fallen world. But at the same time, this psalm ends with "a particularly remarkable and extensive act of praise. There is thus a tension in the psalm."[11] Psalm 22 holds together both the brutally honest expression of a sense of abandonment (Ps 22:1–21) and an extensive thanksgiving to God for his commitment expressed toward his people, both now and in the future (Ps 22:22–31). Psalm 22 clings to two seemingly contradictory ideas: that God has abandoned and that God's commitment is unwavering. This psalm "offers a most suggestive concrete expression of a mature spirituality that is able under pressure to hold on to two contradictory sets of facts."[12] Scripture models a spirituality that is able to trust in God even when the experience of abandonment is undeniable.

Christians are sometimes surprised to learn that more than one-third of all the psalms have the form of a lament.[13] About sixty of the psalms in Scripture are laments. These psalms express abandonment, and this raw expression of pain in the midst of suffering is a regular part of Scripture. Lament is a very common poetic form of prayer to God and even worship of God. This kind of poetry is even the most dominant, in terms of the amount of space devoted to it, of the entire collection of worship poetry in the psalms. And this honest, painful lament is not restricted to the psalms. Job's lament, for example, is direct and blunt when he cries out to God, "Therefore I will not restrain my mouth; I will speak in the anguish of my spirit; I will complain in the bitterness of my soul" (Job 7:10). Scripture includes the frequent and brutally honest prayer to God in the midst of excruciating pain and suffering. This is a significant observation because it clearly suggests that the honest, painful expression of lament to the Lord is intended *by the Lord himself* to be a regular and significant part of our prayer to the Lord and our worship of him.

As mentioned previously, I found the experience of cancer to be very lonely. It was surprising to me how often I felt as though I were facing this illness on my own. But I never spoke of this then to my wife or to anyone else. Even now, I hesitate to write about this sense of loneli-

11. Ibid., 323.

12. Ibid., 340.

13. Fee and Stuart, *How to Read the Bible for All Its Worth*, 212.

ness because I do not want to offend or hurt anyone, especially my wife, because she has done so much for me, and she continues to do so much for me. It is hard for me to imagine another person doing more for me or loving me more. Why is this? Why this hesitation to speak and to write openly and honestly? Perhaps I fear the offense that this would cause—the response from others that they are doing their very best to help and to express compassion to me. Or perhaps I am merely making the natural allowance for human fallibility; such brutal honesty is more than any human should be expected to bear. Or perhaps I am very much afraid that, with my honest expression of pain, I will hurt the very ones who are closest to me, and this is the last thing I ever want to do.

Is it possible that I sometimes treat the Lord as though he is a mere mortal? Do I refrain from the honest expression of lament because, whether I admit it or not, I am afraid that this honesty would be too much to bear, even for God?[14] When I read the lament psalms in Scripture, I do not ever get the sense that the authors of these psalms thought this about God. Instead, lament psalms seem to assume that the Lord is big enough and strong enough to bear the completely honest expression of my lament.

Do we treat God like a fallible human—someone we would not want to hurt with our honest expression of pain? If we do so, we are not treating God as God, but as a mere mortal. I have learned that when I am in the midst of the most excruciating, gut-wrenching pain that seems more than I can endure, one important way to be God-honoring and worshipful to him is to pour out my soul with all its pain and misery fully expressed and to call out to him honestly in my experience of pain because he is the source of my hope, my help, and my life. When I do this, I am confessing my trust in God, my sustainer. If I refrain from lament in the midst of pain, I may actually belittle God and treat him as something less than God; when I follow the example of Scripture and pour out my heart to the Lord in lament, I am engaging in an act of worship.

> *August 7, 2005*
> *I'm awake again. Is it still all really true? When in heaven's name is this nightmare going to go away? I don't want to be a pessimist, but as I was saying last night before my hand just wouldn't move anymore to continue writing, I fear the worst. I have a feeling that*

---

14. Hauerwas, *Naming the Silences*, 83–84.

Jeff is at least in stage three and may have prostate cancer as well or that the Hodgkin's Lymphoma has spread so much that it has gone to his organs. Then I don't know what that means about the treatment. The oncologist said that, depending on what the lump in his groin is and results of the biopsy of the prostate, "it will drastically change his treatment." Does that mean he may be in stage four and they don't treat that? Well, I'm very nervous that this is the answer. So, I don't sleep well anymore. I did OK last night.

3

God's Plan (Now)

For we do not want you to be ignorant, brothers, of the affliction we experienced in Asia. For we were so utterly burdened beyond our strength that we despaired of life itself. Indeed, we felt that we had received the sentence of death. But that was to make us rely not on ourselves but on God who raises the dead.

—2 CORINTHIANS 1:8–9

August 11, 2005
This week, I've been able to get a better handle on myself . . . I think. Through everything I've read—the book I'm reading on Corrie ten Boom's life,[1] *Our Daily Bread and my Bible—I feel God is surrounding me with his love. Even the songs I've heard on the radio. I've been reminded of his grace through my faith. I've tried to write down special Scriptures and excerpts from Pam Moore's book. I've kept whole pages of Our Daily Bread. God is real and he will show himself if you ask him to. Praise God and all glory be to him!*

August 14, 2005
The nightmare gets worse! Friday, the news came that the "thief" has moved into Jeff's bone marrow! He is in stage four! It will only get worse if the prostate tests positive for cancer and/or a tumor has wrapped around the bones in his back . . . and they tell us that there's no use treating him. Jeff's life has become very fragile in the last month!
"What's happening, Heavenly Father?"
This week is going to be crazy and scary. Tomorrow he will undergo the prostate biopsy. Tuesday he has a heart test called a M.U.G.A.

1. Moore, *Life Lessons from the Hiding Place.*

On the same day, he will have the lymph node in his groin removed. Wednesday morning he begins his first chemo treatment. And on Thursday, Jeff will undergo a lung function test. On top of all this, on Wednesday I'm supposed to go to Massachusetts to help Megan move into college. How on earth can I possibly go? How on earth can I possibly leave Megan alone at this time? I'm torn in two, needing and wanting to be in two places at one time.

I believe that Scripture teaches that God is sovereign, and yet he continues to allow his people to live in a world scarred with suffering. *Why?* This is the question that burns in the midst of pain and suffering. The question we ask now is *why?* Can I know the answer to this question, either now or in the future? I am not so sure about this anymore. I certainly can see glimpses of how God has used this horrible experience both in my own life and in the lives of others. Yet there will always be aspects of the impact of this experience that will remain hidden from me. If I were ever to know the reason for this suffering in the ultimate, exhaustive sense, I would need to be omniscient; thus, only God knows why and only God can know why.

Actually, the Bible rarely, if ever, encourages us to ask this question. It assumes that the answer to this question is that we live in a fallen world.[2] Scripture sometimes gives us insight into how God uses suffering, both in the present and also the future. When I discuss God's plan now and in the future, this discussion is based on what God has revealed to us in Scripture. There is no special claim to insight here; only the attempt to discern what Scripture says about suffering in God's plan and purpose for his people. The more important question in Scripture, especially in the lament psalms, is How long?[3] The question is not merely how much longer I must endure this specific experience of suffering. This was my question during my illness. Rather, how much longer must we live in the midst of a fallen world that will inevitably and eventually bring suffering our way? In my reading of Scripture, there are two basic questions that we need to ask in relation to suffering: How is God using this in my life, and how much longer must I endure this?

In his second letter to the Corinthians, Paul gives us insight into an answer to the first question—How does God use suffering in the lives of

2. Hafemann, *The God of Promise and the Life of Faith*, 61–81; and Carson, *How Long, O Lord?* 41–49.

3. Carson, *How Long, O Lord?*

+ How can it glorify HIM?

his people? Paul recounts a time when he faced death (2 Cor 1:8–11). He is not very specific about when or where it was and what he faced; instead, he focuses on what he learned through this time. And lest we think of Paul as an ivory-tower theologian who is detached from the realities of life and its pain and suffering, he remembers "the affliction we experienced in Asia" (v. 8). The word translated here as "affliction" is translated elsewhere in Scripture as "tribulation." This time of trouble resulted in his sense of being utterly burdened beyond his strength with the result that he despaired of life itself (v. 9). He felt as though a death sentence had been pronounced, perhaps even the pronouncement of an official death sentence about which we are otherwise unaware. In any case, it seemed certain to him that he would die.[4]

Paul was in real trouble and facing an imminent death, but God delivered him. This divine deliverance had three results in Paul's own life and in the lives of other Christians:

> For we do not want you to be ignorant, brothers, of the affliction we experienced in Asia. For we were so utterly burdened beyond our strength that we despaired of life itself. Indeed, we felt that we had received the sentence of death. But that was to make us rely not on ourselves but on God who raises the dead. He delivered us from such a deadly peril, and he will deliver us. On him we have set our hope that he will deliver us again. You also must help us by prayer, so that many will give thanks on our behalf for the blessing granted us through the prayers of many. (2 Cor 1:8–11)

First, Paul learned to rely on and trust in God, who is able to raise the dead. Certainly he was a man of faith before this experience, but his faith in God and God's divine power to sustain him grew in and through this time of suffering and impending death. Paul grew to trust in God's goodness and grace, even if he died. He was persuaded to rely on and trust in God so that even if he had, in fact, died, Paul would continue to trust in God. Death itself could not shake his reliance on God. God's resurrection of Jesus Christ demonstrated his power to raise the dead, and this sustained Paul's faith and hope even in the face of death. Death itself could not call into question God's promises and his commitment to act on Paul's behalf. When God sustained him through suffering and pain and even rescued him from it, he learned to trust him even more.[5]

---

4. Hafemann, *2 Corinthians*, 64.

5. Ibid., 64–65.

Second, Paul grew in his hope for the future. God rescued him in the past, and he banked his hope for his future rescue on the God whose past deliverance demonstrated his divine character and commitment to his promise. A little grammar here may be helpful; the tense of the verb in verse 10 that is translated "we have set our hope" indicates there is an abiding quality to this hope. Hafemann helps us to see the theological significance of Paul's description of his time of affliction: "God rescued Paul in the *past* so that he might trust in God's future rescue while he suffered in the *present*" (1:10).[6] God demonstrated his desire to bless Paul in the past, and this had the result in the present of producing the fruit of hope, even in the midst of suffering.

And third, others who were praying for Paul had the opportunity to give thanks to God, who granted him this blessing of rescue from seemingly certain death. Other members of Paul's ministry team and churches he had planted evidently prayed for him. When God rescued Paul and blessed him, these Christians had the opportunity to thank the God who had delivered Paul. Thus God received glory and honor as God rescued him from suffering. God used even this time of extreme suffering and near certain death to honor and glorify himself as the one who sustained and delivered Paul.

God rescued Paul from a time of great suffering in which he thought he was about to die and during which he reached a place of despair. Through this experience, God taught Paul to trust him more and to bank his hope for the future more firmly on him and his promises. And Paul's experience in Asia gave others the opportunity to give thanks to the Lord when he rescued Paul. A possible implication of this passage from Scripture is that God allowed Paul to go through this suffering in order for these things to occur. This is seemingly a clear implication, but is not actually stated here. In the narrative of the raising of Lazarus in John 11, however, this is clearly and explicitly stated as part of the reason for Lazarus's death and the resultant suffering of his sisters (and even for Lazarus himself!).

In John 11, Lazarus was ill and his sisters, Mary and Martha, sent word to Jesus about their brother's condition. When Jesus heard about this, he intentionally stayed where he was for two days until Lazarus had died (v. 5). Why did he do this? Why did he intentionally allow Lazarus to die? Why did he put Mary, Martha, and Lazarus—whom he loved (vv.

6. Ibid., 76. Italics are the author's.

3, 36)—through this suffering and pain? Some of those who witnessed this also asked this very question: "But some of them said, 'Could not he who opened the eyes of the blind man also have kept this man from dying?'" (John 11:37). Bruce writes, "Some indeed thought, and not unnaturally, that such a healer as he had already shown himself to be might have done something to prevent his friend from dying."[7] Indeed Jesus could have kept Lazarus from death, but he chose to delay his arrival in response to this family's request for help until Lazarus had died.

Why did Jesus delay? Jesus certainly was not indifferent to them and their need because John's narrative stresses his compassion for them: "he was deeply moved in his spirit" (v. 33), "he wept" (v. 35), and he was "deeply moved again" (v. 38). Jesus delayed and allowed Lazarus to die in order to display the glory of God so that the Son of God might be glorified through this situation. This point is clearly stated in John's narrative: "So the sisters sent to him, saying, 'Lord, he whom you love is ill.' But when Jesus heard it he said, 'This illness does not lead to death. It is for the glory of God, so that the Son of God may be glorified through it'" (John 11:3–4). Jesus delayed in his response to the sisters' request so that Lazarus might die. This illness would not lead to death as the final word for Lazarus, even though he was to die before Jesus even began to travel to Lazarus's hometown. The glory of God was to be demonstrated as Jesus raised Lazarus from the dead.[8]

Jesus also delayed in order to produce trust in the disciples themselves. Lazarus was allowed to die so that the disciples could learn faith lessons about Jesus. And this faith lesson for the disciples made Jesus glad: "Then Jesus told them plainly, 'Lazarus has died, and for your sake I am glad that I was not there, so that you may believe'" (John 11:14). Jesus allowed suffering and pain for others—Lazarus and his sisters—to demonstrate who he was so that the disciples might grow in their trust in him; Bruce states this clearly, "Jesus implies that, if he had been present in Bethany, Lazarus would not have died. As it is, however, the disciples will see such a manifestation of the glory of God as will kindle their faith, and for that he is glad."[9] The pain and suffering of one family was permitted so that another group might have the opportunity to grow in

---

7. Bruce, *Gospel of John*, 246.

8. Ibid., 240.

9. Ibid., 242.

faith. At least in this one instance in Scripture, God allowed suffering and pain to encourage other people to trust the Lord.

I was diagnosed at the end of the summer break for Oak Hills Christian College. I was to begin my second year of teaching at this college when I learned that I had six to eight months of chemotherapy ahead of me. The college administration very graciously allowed me to remain on full-time status while I took a reduced teaching load. I knew this was necessary in August, but assumed that if I dropped one class from my schedule, I could manage to teach three classes in the fall semester. I was very naïve about what was ahead of me. The administration's suggestion in August was that I teach one or perhaps two classes—a freshman class on interpretive method and a section of Koine Greek, which would be a very small class. I was encouraged to teach one of these, but I chose to teach both.

When October came, I began to question my decision. The cumulative impact of the chemotherapy that I received every two weeks was beginning to take its toll. After this treatment ended, one of the oncology nurses told me that the doctor was very aggressive in his treatment of my disease, given my young family and my relatively young age. She said the doctor was coming at my cancer very aggressively because he was going for life—my life. I had sensed this aggression during my treatment. Cancer and chemo were progressively wearing me down. During the fall semester, I reached a place where I was not sure if I could continue, but I wanted to try to maintain contact with students, especially for my own sake. But when the offer came to teach only one course in the spring, I quickly and gladly agreed!

I wanted to stay in the classroom as much as possible. Some days it was a great struggle just to muster up the energy to get out of the house (on some days this was impossible), but contact with students was a great help to me, both in my mind and in my spirit. It also helped that my wife sat in on my Greek class as a student of this language—something she had previously expressed a desire to do, but this also allowed her to keep an eye on me! I was grateful for her companionship in this class during these days.

My appearance grew increasingly thin and haggard. My wife cut my hair short—to about a half of an inch—because I grew tired of its painfully slow departure on my pillow and down the shower drain. As this hair slowly and progressively thinned, a staff person at the college remarked once that I looked like a Charlie Brown character. I grew pale and thin. My legs began to lose their strength, and I began to have difficulty walking. I was constantly tired. It is the oddest experience to wake up from a three-hour nap more tired than when the nap began. My body slowly began to wear down under the weight of the treatment for my cancer.

As my physical appearance slowly deteriorated over the weeks and months of chemotherapy, I was very much aware that students at the college were watching me go through this experience. This is naturally a part of the Christian college experience at Oak Hills as faculty and students are encouraged to enter into mentoring and discipleship relationships; frankly, in my opinion, instructors perhaps gain the most from these relationships. But this particular experience was unique as students watched me battle a deadly disease. I was aware that my responses to this pain and suffering were observed, but after a while, I really could not care about this. My reactions and responses were what they were. Yet I hoped others saw God's grace which sustained me through these dark days.

In my recent conversations with some who saw me go through this, it is apparent that God used my suffering to help others who saw him work on my behalf through this suffering. God helped them to grow in faith and hope in and through the intense suffering that I endured. One staff person at the college once remarked about her admiration of my great courage as I battled cancer. This statement actually stunned me. I didn't know how to respond to this. The memory of this remark has always been very humbling for me because I never, ever thought of my responses during my illness as particularly heroic, noble, or courageous. In fact, I often thought of myself as quite the opposite—fear often stalked me and seemingly was about to consume me. Discouragement was my constant companion. Yet God apparently used my suffering, as he graciously sustained me through it, to be an encouragement to others to trust him more and more. The cancer and its pain and suffering were not a good thing, but this was a very good thing, in my view. God, the gracious giver of the good gifts, which sustained me through suffering, was glorified in his people as they grew to trust him more. God sometimes allows his people to suffer in the midst of a fallen world to teach them to trust him, and he also uses suffering to glorify himself when he sustains and, at times, delivers his people.

Scripture teaches that God uses suffering in the lives of believers to teach them to trust him; Scripture also teaches that God uses suffering to build Christian character in them. In Romans, for example, we read:

> Therefore, since we have been justified by faith, we have peace
> with God through our Lord Jesus Christ. Through him we have
> also obtained access by faith into this grace in which we stand,
> and we rejoice in hope of the glory of God. More than that, we
> rejoice in our sufferings, knowing that suffering produces endur-
> ance, and endurance produces character, and character produces
> hope, and hope does not put us to shame, because God's love
> has been poured into our hearts through the Holy Spirit who has
> been given to us. (Rom 5:1–5)

I did my very first interpretation paper in my college Greek class
on the first half of Romans 5, so this passage holds a place of special
fondness for me! I remember my surprise when I read that "we rejoice
in our sufferings"! Suffering and rejoicing did not seem to go together so
much in my mind then. But when we keep reading, we notice that this
rejoicing in our sufferings is the result of what God does in us through
our sufferings; he produces endurance in us and also builds character in
us. We are able to rejoice, even in sufferings, when we see the work that
God is doing to build character in us.[10]

I also remember that I noticed that this truth from God's word was
bracketed by the word *hope*, at the end of verse 2: "and we rejoice in the
hope of the glory of God," and at the end of verse 4: "and character produces hope." This part of Scripture thus begins and ends with the statement of the hope of God's glory, and this is the hope that is produced in
us through endurance and through character-building experiences. And
as hope for the future in the midst of the suffering of this world enables
endurance and produces character, hope is enhanced and strengthened.
Moo writes about this tension between suffering and hope: "paradoxi-
cally, Paul claims at the end of verse 4, suffering can actually lead to
'hope.' Just as resistance to a muscle strengthens it, so challenges to our
hope can strengthen it."[11] This movement from hope through suffering
to hope is like a spiral in which this newly strengthened hope then further enables endurance and produces more character in us. And this
hope then continues to grow our Christian endurance and character
throughout our lives. The spiral of God's work in our life moves from
hope to endurance to character and back to hope again.

10. Moo, *Romans*, 170–71.
11. Ibid., 171.

And this Christian hope will not disappoint us because God has already poured out his love and his Spirit upon us. We see once again in Scripture the very real and abiding presence of God inspiring endurance in the present and producing hope for the future! God uses the suffering that we experience in this fallen world to produce endurance, build character, and inspire hope. This hope is a confident expectation both because the God who has promised is faithful, because he has already poured out his love upon us, even in the midst of suffering, and he has already given us the gift of the Holy Spirit—the gift of his indwelling presence.[12] The God who has promised to work for us in the future has already begun to work for us in the present. When we rejoice in this hope, we are able even more to rejoice in our sufferings. God uses suffering to build Christian character in us. We can learn to trust him more and more as we endure suffering.[13]

The second question that we often ask in the midst of suffering is, How much longer must I endure this? Although a fuller answer to this question is the task of the next chapter, one aspect of its answer can be explored here. To anticipate this fuller answer, Scripture promises that God's plan for the future is a new heaven and a new earth in which the impact of sin and death will be dealt with once and for all.[14] This fallen world, with its pain and suffering, will be restored to God's intention so that sin and death will be removed. Yet now we await the fulfillment of this promise in hope.

> God may heal, here and now, but not on every occasion. There may be occasions, here and now, when evil powers are defeated, but not always. This should not surprise us. The present evil age will eventually give way to the next. If we all received from God complete holiness and wholeness now, there would be no need for the new earth. As it is, however, we live on an earth presently controlled by the evil one. Only when Satan is finally defeated shall we know life as God intended it.[15]

In the New Creation death will be defeated and destroyed (1 Cor 15:20–28), and pain and suffering will be no more (Rev 21:3–4).

---

12. Ibid., 171–72.
13. Carson, *How Long, O Lord?* 229–46.
14. Alexander, *From Eden to the New Jerusalem.*
15. Ibid., 155.

So if this is God's plan for the future, how much longer must I endure this? Why the delay? Why not now? The instruction recorded in
2 Peter 3:1–13 concerning the Day of the Lord and the return of Jesus
Christ may make an important contribution to an answer to this question. This contribution to an answer to the question of how long must we
endure suffering in a fallen world is not directly stated in this passage,
but it is an inference drawn from it. Moreover, this inference does not
answer the question in relation to my particular experience of suffering
in any given circumstance in life, but rather it answers the question of
how much longer we must live in a fallen world in which suffering and
pain are possible. In other words, this passage does not answer the question of how much longer we must endure suffering in any particular circumstance; but rather, how much longer must we live in a fallen world. If
God's plan is to remove us from the curse of a fallen world and to restore
us in a new heaven and a new earth, why does he not act to do so today?
Why the delay in the establishment of the New Creation in which death,
pain, and suffering are not possible? Why the delay?

In 2 Peter, some false prophets and false teachers have infiltrated
the Christian community to which this letter is addressed. These false
teachers are identified by their greed and their immoral behavior (2 Pet
2),[16] and they probably are preaching that Jesus Christ is not really coming back physically and thus there is no future judgment. Their preaching emphasizes that there is no future consequence for present behavior.
2 Peter reminds its readers both of the Lord's commandments and the
predictions of those who would scoff at his return (2 Pet 3:1–4). They
ask, "Where is this promised return?" It has been so long! Yet these false
prophets and false teachers "deliberately forget" that God is creator of
this world, has judged it before in the days of Noah, and is not slow in
keeping his promises (2 Pet 3:5–9). God's past actions clearly demonstrate that he is willing and able to judge the unrepentant. The evident
delay in the promised return of Jesus Christ is due to God's patience and
mercy toward the rebellious and unrepentant.

> But do not overlook this one fact, beloved, that with the Lord one
> day is as a thousand years, and a thousand years as one day. The
> Lord is not slow to fulfill his promise as some count slowness,
> but is patient toward you, not wishing that any should perish, but
> that all should reach repentance. (2 Pet 3:9–10)

16. Moo, *2 Peter, Jude*, 125–29.

Instead, God's apparent delay that these false teachers have taken to mean his indifference toward moral behavior is rather a sign of his great patience toward those who need to repent.

The Day of the Lord is coming like a thief, and judgment day is sure and certain (2 Pet 3:10). This verse states that on this day, "the works that are done on it [i.e., the earth] will be exposed." The implication of this passage is not that God is indifferent to his fallen creation and the behavior of its people. This is the inference falsely drawn by these false teachers and false prophets.

> But the word "some" has a polemical edge. It is more likely that Peter is thinking of the false teachers themselves. They view the delay in the fulfillment of God's promise as a sign of God's weakness or uninvolvement with history. God is not really concerned with what is happening here on earth, they may have argued, so that any idea of a real end of the world or of judgment is foolish.[17]

The implication, instead, is that God is patient even with unbelieving scoffers whom he desires to give more opportunity for repentance. Meanwhile, believers are to live in holiness and godliness and with patience as they wait for God to keep his promises. As they live such lives, they in some way "hasten" or "wait eagerly" for the arrival of this promised day.[18] This growth in godliness is an important theme in 2 Peter; this letter begins with a description of its importance for entrance into the kingdom (2 Pet 1:1–11), and it ends with the command to grow in grace (2 Pet 3:18). Believers now are to grow in grace and to wait patiently for God to keep his promises. In this way they demonstrate their eagerness for God's promises to be realized and they also in some way speed its arrival. God's people are indeed saved in hope (Rom 8:24–25).[19]

God's delay in Christ's return and the restoration of this fallen creation is his patience, and this patience is an expression of his mercy toward unbelief. God allows the saints to live in a fallen world in which they experience suffering and pain in order to give even unrepentant scoffers more opportunity for repentance because he desires none to perish in the judgment to come when Christ returns. Thus God's delay

17. Ibid., 187.

18. Ibid., 198.

19. Hafemann, *The God of Promise and the Life of Faith*, 107–28.

in the establishment of the New Creation in which death, pain, and suffering are eradicated forever is evangelistic!

Why the delay? How much longer must we endure the pain and suffering that come to us in the midst of a fallen world? We must wait with patience and eagerness until Christ returns to establish a new heaven and a new earth. And his apparent delay is not indifference toward the immoral behavior of unbelieving scoffers, nor is it indifference toward the suffering of the saints. It is his mercy and patience, which is giving more and more opportunity for repentance. The inference that I have drawn from this passage is that the present endurance of the saints in a fallen world has the divine intention of the continued opportunity for repentance for unbelievers. And in some mysterious way, Christians' growth in godliness and holiness along with their patient and eager waiting for God to fulfill his promises help to speed the appearance of this great Day of the Lord. As we wait patiently, even through severe pain and suffering, and as we desire to see very soon the New Creation in which pain and suffering are removed forever, may we grow in holiness and in godliness. And as a scoffing and unbelieving world observes our tenacious and unrelenting grasp on God and his promises, may they be granted repentance before the great judgment on the Day of the Lord. Maranatha!

> *August 14, 2005*
> *God, I need your strength and wisdom in knowing what to do. God, show me what you want me to do when it comes to the time that I need to travel to Massachusetts to help Megan move into college. I feel I need to go, but I need to be here for Jeff and the children! I have to go—I have to stay home! Send some help, God! Amen.*

4

God's Plan (In the Future)

And I heard a loud voice from the throne saying, "Behold, the dwelling place of God is with man. He will dwell with them, and they will be his people, and God himself will be with them as their God. He will wipe away every tear from their eyes, and death shall be no more, neither shall there be mourning, nor crying, nor pain anymore, for the former things have passed away."

—REVELATION 21:3–4

August 16, 2005

Yesterday was Jeff's prostate biopsy. The doctor was so nice, and I was allowed to stay with him. I'm so glad! It wasn't too painful but not very comfortable. The doctor said Jeff's prostate looked good. Now we can only hope for the best news from the test results . . . that it is normal. That news will come while I'm gone to Massachusetts!

I'm due to leave the house at 6:45 a.m. to catch a 12:30 p.m. plane from Minneapolis. Maggie is driving me down. Jeff is starting chemo at 8:30 a.m. with labs first. Dan is going to take Jeff to the oncologist and stay with him for the day. Cheryl has come from Nebraska to stay and to take care of my family while I'm away. I'm so thankful someone is going with Jeff, and Cheryl will be here with the kids. Praise God! He is providing three of me! One to be with Megan, one to be with Jeff, and one to be with the children! I still want to be in all three places, but God is providing for us.

"So, Father, thank you so much for your sustaining love."

August 17, 2005

I'm at 32,000 feet on my way to Boston. Leaving this morning was one of the most difficult things I've ever done—without a doubt. As Maggie drove me to Minneapolis, Jeff was receiving his first chemo treatment. He was there at 8:30 a.m., and got home some time be-

39

fore 3 p.m. Dan called me three times to let me know Jeff was doing well. No side effects during the injections. The nurse said the next three days will be tough—I wonder if he's planning on preaching this Sunday? His hair is going to fall out. Maybe even before his next treatment in two weeks.

I can't believe this is happening to my husband! I'm still having a nightmare, right? Someone, please wake me up!

Everyone keeps telling me they know someone with this kind of cancer. And that they were stage four. And that they are healed now. I know they are trying to comfort me, but I have to be real. That "thief" is in his bone marrow. I don't know the results of the prostate biopsy. The lymph node in his groin is still not diagnosed, and what's the mass near or on the bone in his back? I still have so many unanswered questions.

Scripture begins with God's creation of the world and his pronouncement that it is very good. Sin and death enter the picture for humanity through their own willful rebellion against God (Gen 1–3). Scripture concludes with the description of the promise of the New Heaven and the New Earth (Rev 21–22). In many important ways, everything in between this beginning and ending for Scripture is the unfolding story of how God intends to move humanity from this rebellious beginning with its painful consequences to his intention to set the world right again and undo the damage done through humanity's rebellion against him. This unfolding story reaches its climax and conclusion in the New Creation.[1]

Scripture teaches that God is sovereign, and yet he continues to allow his people to live in a world scarred with suffering. Why? This is the overwhelming and consuming question in the midst of suffering. Why? Can I know the answer? Now? Ever? In the last chapter I suggested that God uses suffering now in order to teach lessons of trust in him, and God continues to allow suffering in a fallen world to provide scoffing unbelievers time to repent. This gives us a glimpse into how God uses suffering now, but I am not sure we should so boldly and confidently proclaim that we know the answer to this question. There are certainly many people influenced and impacted by suffering for whom God works this together for good. Many certainly grow in trust as they patiently endure suffering or observe the patient endurance of others.[2] But there are

1. Alexander, *From Eden to New Jerusalem*; Wright, *Evil and the Justice of God*; and Carson, *How Long, O Lord?* 133–51.

2. Hafemann, *The God of Promise and the Life of Faith,* 149–65.

pieces to the puzzle of God's plan that may always be hidden to us. There are ways that God uses suffering to which I am completely blind—and I may never see them. Ultimately, we can know, in part, how God uses suffering, but to know why in some comprehensive sense I would need to be omniscient—I would need to be God. And this I will never be. So in response to the question of why a sovereign God continues to allow his people to live in a world scarred with suffering, we can only know in part some of the ways God uses suffering to teach lessons of faith, and we can trust in his plan for the future.

Although we often ask the question of why God allows suffering, Scripture's clear and consistent response is that we live in a fallen world. Sometimes we ask *why* when we really want to know *how* God uses suffering. The previous chapter suggested some ways in which God may use suffering now, and in this chapter we will explore God's plan for the future. In biblical theology the more important question, more important than why or how God is using this particular experience now, is *how long?*[3] The question is not merely how much longer must we endure a specific experience of suffering, but rather, how much longer must we live in the midst of a fallen world that will inevitably and eventually bring suffering our way.

A full description of God's plan for the future as Scripture describes it is beyond the scope of this book. We will look instead at how this plan is introduced in the call of Abram (Gen 12:1–3) and how God's plan culminates in the climax of the canon of Scripture in a new heaven and a new earth (Rev 21–22). In Genesis, God calls Abram in order to bless his future and the future of his family, and this future blessing includes the blessing of all the families of the earth. God's blessing of everyone impacted by this fallen world is an important part of his plan from the start. And this plan reaches its fulfillment in the description of the New Creation in Revelation as all the nations enjoy the benefit and the blessing of the restoration of God's creation.

After the fall described in Genesis 3 and the outworking of the impact of that fall for humanity and for God's creation, God calls Abraham. The narrative prior to this call includes the story of the flood in divine response to humanity's rebellion (Gen 4–11) and the dispersion of the nations at Babel, which is also a divine judgment (Gen 11:1–9). The narrative of Genesis emphasizes that humanity's rebellion against God and

3. Carson, *How Long, O Lord?*

the consequent divine judgment is increasing and extending throughout God's creation. This is an ironic reversal of God's intention for his creation. God created humanity to fill and exercise dominion over creation, but instead humanity fills the earth with increasing rebellion and the resulting divine judgment on this rebellion. In response to this increasing rebellion, God calls Abraham to leave his homeland and go to a land that God himself will show him (Gen 12:1–3).

God's promises to him in this call include the promise that "in you all the families of the earth shall be blessed." This promise, with some modification, is repeated to Abraham and to his sons in the patriarchal narrative (Gen 18:18; 22:18; 26:4; and 28:14). Perhaps the most significant modification in the repeated promise to Abraham is the variation in these five passages between "all families" and "all the nations," phrases that probably have basically the same meaning. Part of God's intention through Abraham's call is to bless all the families and all the nations of the earth. God's call of Abraham is an act of divine mercy in response to humanity's rebellion at Babel, and it is a renewal of God's intention for humanity since the beginning.

> We have already suggested that by placing the call of Abraham after the dispersion of the nations at Babylon (11:1–9), the author intends to picture Abraham's call as God's gift of salvation in the midst of judgment. As a way of sustaining this theme even further, the author has patterned the account of Abraham's call and blessing after an earlier account of a similar gift of salvation in the midst of judgment, the conclusion of the Flood narrative. . . . The similarities between the two narratives are striking and show that Abraham, like Noah, marks a new beginning as well as a return to God's original plan of blessing "all humankind" (1:28).[4]

Although the specific way they are to be blessed is not clearly stated at all here, it is clear that God's intention for good in his call of Abraham includes blessing for every nation on earth. God's plan for the future thus is inclusive of all of humanity.

And Scripture asserts that God has begun to fulfill this promise of blessing for the nations. Those who trust in Christ are justified in fulfillment of God's promise to Abraham: "And the Scripture, foreseeing that God would justify the Gentiles by faith, preached the gospel beforehand to Abraham, saying, 'In you shall all the nations be blessed'" (Gal 3:8).

---

4. Sailhamer, *The Pentateuch as Narrative*, 139.

Paul quotes the promise to Abraham in Genesis and claims that it is ful-filled for those gentiles who trust in Christ. Significantly, Paul asserts that this promise of blessing for Gentiles through faith in Christ is the gospel preached beforehand. Gentiles who trust in Christ have received the blessing promised to Abraham, and they even have received Abraham's blessing (Gal 3:14). This blessing of Gentiles comes through Abraham's "seed" or "descendant," who is Christ. This fulfillment of the promise to Abraham of blessing for the nations through a descendant of Abraham is anticipated at the close of the narrative in Genesis when Jacob predicts that a descendant of Judah will rule and receive tribute and obedience from the nations (Gen 49:8–10).[5] Gentiles are blessed through Abraham and are also included in Abraham's family (Gal 3:25–29). God's promise to bless all of humanity through faith in Christ has already begun in and through the gospel of Jesus Christ.

When the end of the story of God's plan to restore creation is reached in Revelation, it is therefore no surprise that his intentions in-clude all of humanity. The description of a new heaven and a new earth as the New Jerusalem descends to earth includes a proclamation of the blessing of God's presence for humanity: "And I heard a loud voice from the throne saying, 'Behold, the dwelling place of God is with man. He will dwell with them, and they will be his people, and God himself will be with them as their God'" (Rev 21:3). This promise of God's dwelling with humanity here is likely intended to echo the promise of blessing for the nations.[6] Moreover, this blessing of God's presence for humanity removes pain and suffering from their experience: "He will wipe away every tear from their eyes, and death shall be no more, neither shall there be mourning, nor crying, nor pain anymore, for the former things have passed away" (Rev 21:4). Believers from all nations will enjoy the blessing of this indescribable experience—no more pain and suffering. This is God's intention for all of humanity; the description of the New Jerusalem includes the mention of the nations: "By its light will the na-tions walk, and the kings of the earth will bring their glory into it" (Rev 21:24).[7] The nations will be restored to God's intention for his creation.

---

5. Ibid., 140.

6. Keener, *Revelation*, 487; and Alexander, *From Eden to the New Jerusalem*, 138–70.

7. Keener, *Revelation*, 498–99.

> Then the angel showed me the river of the water of life, bright as crystal, flowing from the throne of God and of the Lamb through the middle of the street of the city; also, on either side of the river, the tree of life with its twelve kinds of fruit, yielding its fruit each month. The leaves of the tree were for the healing of the nations. (Rev 22:1–2)

The New Jerusalem in the New Creation is for all the nations of the earth, and this blessing of the New Creation includes the healing power of the tree of life for the nations, which clearly refers to the tree of life in the garden (Gen 2:9; 3:22) and the tree of healing promised in Scripture (Ezek 47:1–12).[8]

Revelation thus ends where Scripture began. People from all nations are restored to God's creation and are removed from suffering and death. People, whom God created in his image, are restored to the tree of life in the New Creation.

> Whereas Genesis 3 highlights the negative impact of being excluded from the tree of life, John's vision of the New Jerusalem in Revelation 22 includes a description of the tree, echoing an earlier passage in Ezekiel 47:12. Revelation 22 underlines the tree's life-giving power by describing how it produces twelve kinds of fruit—a different fruit every month. The context implies that the tree's leaves renew those who eat them. . . . No one will grow frail by becoming old in the New Jerusalem. Citizens of the new earth will experience and enjoy both wholeness of body and longevity of life. They will have a quality of life unrestricted by disability or disease. To live in the New Jerusalem is to experience life in all its fullness and vitality. It is to live as one has never lived before. It is to be in the prime of life, for the whole of one's life.[9]

The blessing extended to believers from all the nations is also clearly a part of the overall story of Revelation as it progresses to this climax. This is certainly implied in the inclusive blessing pronounced at the beginning and the end of Revelation (1:3; 22:14). A great multitude of the faithful from all the nations is described as standing before the throne (Rev 7:9–17). And a great multitude, presumably from all the nations in light of Revelation 7, is present at the great marriage feast of the Lamb, and the invitation to this feast is a great blessing (Rev 19:6–10).

8. Ibid., 505–8.

9. Alexander, *From Eden to the New Jerusalem*, 156.

God's plan for the future is unveiled in Abraham's call and is realized in a new heaven and a new earth. The unveiling of God's plan makes it clear that he has all of humanity in mind for this time of restoration and blessing in the future. The climax and culmination of this plan for the future explicitly includes a great multitude from every nation—it includes all the families of the earth. This future hope is the restoration of creation with pain and suffering removed from it.

Until that day, believers continue to live in hope in the midst of a fallen world. This world eventually and inevitably is the source of suffering for them, in one form or another. The pain experienced in this fallen world may vary; but it is real, and it comes regularly. Those who trust in God's promised plan for the future live in hope and long for its realization. In Romans 8 creation itself is personified, and it also groans in anticipation of the day when God will remove from it suffering and pain. Creation itself longs for the day when it will be set free from its bondage to corruption and will be restored as the New Creation.

> For I consider that the sufferings of this present time are not worth comparing with the glory that is to be revealed to us. For the creation waits with eager longing for the revealing of the sons of God. For the creation was subjected to futility, not willingly, but because of him who subjected it, in hope that the creation itself will be set free from its bondage to corruption and obtain the freedom of the glory of the children of God. For we know that the whole creation has been groaning together in the pains of childbirth until now. (Rom 8:18–22)

Creation, personified, was subjected to futility because it failed to reach the purpose of its creator.[10] It was subject to the "bondage to corruption" (v. 21), which was the result of the rebellion of humanity against their creator. So creation also looks forward to the day when God will restore it to its intended purpose and function and will free it from its own bondage to corruption and death. This anticipation and groaning is compared to the labor pains of childbirth, which certainly is an intense and painful experience that anticipates the joyful arrival of a newborn child.[11]

---

10. Moo, *Romans*, 267.

11. Ibid.

At the present time, believers have the first fruits of their future redemption in the Spirit, the very presence of God with them as they live in this fallen world:

> And not only the creation, but we ourselves, who have the first-fruits of the Spirit, groan inwardly as we wait eagerly for adoption as sons, the redemption of our bodies. For in this hope we were saved. Now hope that is seen is not hope. For who hopes for what he sees? But if we hope for what we do not see, we wait for it with patience. (Rom 8:23–25)

Those who have the Spirit and who trust in God's promises for the future also groan as they await the day when God will renew our fallen world in a new heaven and a new earth. When God restores this fallen creation, believers will be changed; they will have God's glory revealed in them (v. 18). They will also receive the inheritance in the New Creation that is due to those who have received the adoption as sons (v. 23), and they will receive the redemption of their bodies (v. 23). This is the hope of the resurrection to a glorified body in the New Creation.[12]

Three additional observations are crucial for our topic. First, present suffering in this fallen world cannot compare to the glory promised to believers in the future (Rom 8:18). Present suffering is real and painful, but it is not on the same level as the glory promised to believers in the New Creation. This is no ivory-tower theology from Paul; he knew suffering in his life, perhaps more than most (see, e.g., 2 Cor 11:23–29). But he had also seen the resurrected Jesus on the Damascus Road and knew the surpassing value of the Christian hope of the resurrection and the New Creation.

Second, believers groan inwardly as they suffer in a fallen world, which itself groans under the weight of its bondage to corruption (Rom 8:23). Believers have the first fruits of the Spirit, which means they have the beginning of the restoration of God's abiding presence with them now. First fruits in Scripture indicate the beginning stage of a harvest season in which the first of a fuller crop has already been harvested. This first crop ensures that the fuller harvest is to come in the future— the harvest season has already started. This point is crucial and bears emphasis: it is the beginning of the same harvest season. The present possession and experience of the Spirit is the beginning of the fulfill-

---

12. Wright, *Surprised by Hope.*

ment of God's promise to restore all things. Yet even those who have the first fruits of the Spirit are not exempt from the pain and suffering in a world subjected to corruption. And even those who have the Spirit now groan under the weight of pain and suffering they experience. Stoic endurance of pain and suffering is not a Christian virtue. The honest expression of pain is.

And third, believers wait patiently (Rom 8:24–25). Without this, the honest expression of pain could simply be grumbling and whining. The Christian hope and the believer's patient endurance of suffering in this world in this hope transform this groaning into a statement of faith. This patient endurance is a main thread that runs straight through this passage: "For I do not consider . . ." (v. 18), ". . . in hope . . ." (v. 20), "for we know . . ." (v. 22), ". . . as we wait eagerly . . ." (v.23), "for in this hope . . ." (v. 24; and the word "hope" is used three more times in this verse!), and "but if we hope for what we do not see, we wait for it with patience" (v. 25). Things are not now as they should be, and believers trust that one day God will keep his promises. This is the Christian hope that enables believers to wait patiently and expectantly for God to keep his promises.[13] This faith and hope enable them to trust their future safety and security to God.

This Christian hope is central to the message of the New Testament as it develops and brings to a climax the story of redemption in Scripture. When the Lord returns, our mortal and corruptible bodies will be transformed in the New Creation, and we will have resurrection bodies no longer subject to sin, corruption, and death. This is the Christian hope that the Apostle Paul describes and defends at length in 1 Corinthians 15. In this highly significant passage about the hope of the resurrection, Paul affirms that we are destined for new bodies that will be free from the capacity for corruption and death (1 Cor 15:50–58). Indeed, as Christ vanquishes all foes in the establishment of the kingdom of God, death is the last enemy to be brought into submission (1 Cor 15:20–28). This hope for the resurrection in the New Creation deserves to regain a more prominent place in Christian hope and in the gospel that proclaims this hope. Christian hope ultimately is not of a disembodied, spiritual existence in heaven, but rather of an embodied and eternal existence in a new heaven and a new earth.[14]

13. Moo, *Romans*, 267–68.

14. Wright, *Surprised by Hope*.

It is this hope for which 2 Peter calls us to wait patiently. God may deliver us from suffering now, but he has promised that he will deliver from it in the future—in the New Creation. God does sustain and teach trust in him now, but the day is coming when he will remove all pain and suffering from human experience in a new heaven and a new earth. The New Jerusalem will include the tree of life, whose leaves will be for the healing of the nations. And in both 2 Peter and Revelation, it is the return of Christ to this earth that will result in the establishment of a new heaven and a new earth in which creation is restored and suffering is removed from our human experience. We look forward to this hope, and we even long for it!

When I was in the depths of my treatment for cancer, despair was never far from my footsteps. Some days it seemed endless, until I contemplated the natural end of cancer. Then I would continue to persevere through the pain and fatigue, even though I did not really know that this treatment would cure this disease. But I must confess that, for very selfish reasons, I grew to long for Christ's return like I had never longed for it before. Now I would have said that I lived in eager expectation of his soon return, and I still think that this was my sincerely held belief. But something about the experience of staring my own mortality in the face seemed to intensify this longing for me.

I remember one time when I was leaving the college campus after teaching a single class for that day. I was heading home to take a three-hour nap when I heard a song on a local Christian radio station. This song had Christ's return as its main theme. Frankly, it was hard to listen to this song; I did not want merely the idea of Christ's return that afternoon, but the reality of it. I wanted it to happen now! Then the next song played on the radio, and it too had this same theme—a consideration of Christ's return. At this point, I needed to pull over to the side of the road because I was weeping so much that I could no longer see the road. I thought, why not today? Why not now?

I freely admit that my reaction was selfish because I believe that if Christ had returned that day, my battle with cancer would have been over. If he returned then, all this suffering would be no more. His return would mean that the back pain caused by the Neupogen would end. The fatigue and muscle weakness that haunted my every step would cease. I wanted this so badly on that day that I was consumed with emotion with just the mere thought. The idea that Christ could come on that day overwhelmed my emotions, and I wanted it more than I had ever desired it or ever have since.

He did not return that day, quite obviously! But I continue to trust in God's plan for the future. I endure whatever this life throws my way because I have banked my hope for the future on God's promises, which include especially the hope of the New Creation. Yet the promise of Scripture in Revelation is not that one day I will know the reason behind everything that happens to me, to my family and friends, and ultimately in our fallen world. The promise of Scripture is that God intends to restore this fallen creation, and that on that day he intends to dwell with us, to wipe the tears from our eyes, and to remove death from our experience once and for all:

Why does God allow suffering now? I have learned to leave this with God. Carson's study of the topic of suffering concludes,

> The mystery of providence defies our attempt to tame it by reason. I do not mean it is illogical; I mean that we do not know enough to be able to unpack it and domesticate it. Perhaps we may gauge how content we are to live with our limitations by assessing whether we are comfortable in joining the biblical writers in utterances that mock our frankly idolatrous devotion to our own capacity to understand.[15]

I think that I often overestimate my capacity to know, especially when the question is why. If what I really mean with this question is that I can see in part how God has used this suffering in my life and in the lives of others, then God does allow me to see this from time to time. But if I mean why this has happened in some final and exhaustive sense in all of its connections and details, I have learned to leave this with God. Only God can really know why. Only God is omniscient.

But what about in the future? Will I know the answer to this question in the future, in heaven? I am not so sure anymore. I will perhaps see more clearly how God used suffering for good, but where in Scripture is the promise that I will know everything about every part of every one of my experiences here on this earth along with how all this influenced and impacted everyone I know (and also those I don't know)? I do not see such a promise in Scripture, and I don't think that I will ever be omniscient, even in heaven. Why then have I been so certain that when I get to heaven, I will know why? Perhaps even then I will simply need

15. Carson, *How Long, O Lord?* 226.

to continue to trust in a sovereign, wise, and good God. Even then I will need to be a creature who must trust his creator.

> *August 20, 2005*
>
> *Every day since I've been gone, Jeff has felt increasingly tired and more sick than the day before. I can hear it in his voice. I feel that maybe he's even feeling worse than he lets on over the phone. I'm almost afraid to go home and see him feeling this way. And I'm not looking forward to his hair falling out, because this cancer will be more than head knowledge. I'm afraid for the kids to see this happen.*
>
> *"God give me the grace not to overreact when that happens. Help me deal with it and be supportive of Jeff at every hurdle. Help the children to go through it as well with grace. And help Jeff as he sees his own physical appearance change before his very eyes. We're heading into the worst event that has happened to our little family, and we'll need your grace that is sufficient. Help us draw upon your love and strength."*
>
> *August 22, 2005*
>
> *Back up in the air, I'm on my way home through Chicago. Jeff had a bad night last night. He thinks he ate too much so he couldn't get comfortable. I didn't sleep either. I'm so ready to be home, yet I will miss Megan immensely. She will be fine once she gets into a routine!*
>
> *One of the drugs Jeff is taking causes big mood swings. Last night he snapped at me, and it brought tears to my eyes. At the time I thought it was because he was tired or wasn't feeling well. This morning I asked if he was OK enough to come and get me at the airport. It is a four-hour trip each way. He said he was anxious to get me home; then he had a burst of tears. It's going to be a bumpy road. I'm pretty tired, and I need to be strong when I crawl into the car with Jeff. I'm going to try and nap now.*

PART TWO

Biblical-Theological Reflections on God's Grace Experienced during a Season of Suffering

5

Life Is a Vapor

Come now, you who say, "Today or tomorrow we will go into such and such a town and spend a year there and trade and make a profit"—yet you do not know what tomorrow will bring. What is your life? For you are a mist that appears for a little time and then vanishes.

—JAMES 4:13–14

September 2, 2005
Jeff's white count was too low on the 31ˢᵗ for chemo. We were both disappointed because the chemo works best if received at exact intervals. It will almost be like starting over again. He did have chemo on September 1ˢᵗ. An injection of Neupogen on the 31ˢᵗ really boosted the white count! Now I have to give him these shots at home starting three days after chemo for seven days in a row. They cause so much pain in his bones! I wonder how he will teach? This is going to be a hard year. I will hate giving these to him (not that it's hard to give the shot), because I know they will cause him so much pain! Yet, this will be a tangible way I can help him. I hate cancer!

The white blood count went very low, and as a result, his body was unable to fight off the germs in his mouth so he developed one very nasty sore on his lip. It was nasty! And very painful!

His hair is beginning to fall out. It may be all gone in a week.

September 30, 2005
Jeff was to have chemo yesterday, but he's been too sick this week. He had a temperature of 103.8 ° on Tuesday night. He couldn't even think straight, and he was talking fast—that's when I knew he was bad, and we went to the E.R. He shakes and talks a lot and very fast. The temperature was caused by the Bleomycin. It was causing minor lung damage, thus causing the fever. So, he's off that chemo drug. They say it shouldn't change the effectiveness of the treatment

too much. We'll be interested to see what side effects he won't go through now!

In this second section I will describe some of the lessons that I learned during this time of suffering. Now I would have said that I already knew these before my struggle with this dreaded disease. I do not consider any of the discussion of these topics in this section novel or unique. But I did learn some surprising aspects of these well-known truths from Scripture during this walk through a very dark valley. As a result, these lessons for me were not necessarily learned for the first time during this period of my life, but instead some basic truths from Scripture had the opportunity to grow deeper roots into my life. I continue to grow in these areas.

Life is short. There is not very much that is terribly profound here! But I must confess that I have often lived my life as though I were here on this earth forever. I would profess with my lips this truth from Scripture, but my behaviors often suggested otherwise. Even though I knew that life is short and that I am not here on this earth forever, I often made choices without much, if any, consideration of the brevity of my life. In this attitude and in these behaviors I am certainly not alone.

> Menaced by abortion and genetic dysfunction before we are born, by sickness and accident at any moment of our lives, by old age and death at the end of our lives—the wonder is not that we realize we are fragile and vulnerable, but that at any time we ever fall for the conceit that we are not. Yet many people in their late teens and early twenties live as if they will live forever, and many of us who are older act, talk, and joke as if to perpetuate the illusion.[1]

If we are honest with ourselves, most of us actually live our lives as though we will really be here on this earth forever after all. Most of us travel through life, most of the time at least, as though we will live forever. The fragile nature of our lives and the basic fact of our mortality are not topics we care to consider very much or very often, and they are generally best ignored in day-to-day living.[2]

Those who claim Christian faith and hope may profess one thing, but a life lived in awareness of and response to this basic truth of life in a fallen world is another thing altogether. The value of living life with

---

1. Guinness, *Unspeakable*, 20.
2. Ibid., 19–33.

its end in view has largely been lost in our day, even for Christians.[3] For me, it really did not seem to matter whether the consequences appeared to be great or small. Certainly I was aware that my life is not unending, but this often remained on the periphery of my thoughts as I lived my daily, routine, everyday life. Rarely, if ever, did it become central to my thoughts when I made choices in daily living.

Life is short. This is the basic message of James when he teaches on this topic. James reminds us of the brevity of life and warns us of the danger that comes along with the presumption and arrogance of the person who thinks that he lives in self-sufficient independence.

> Come now, you who say, "Today or tomorrow we will go into such and such a town and spend a year there and trade and make a profit"—yet you do not know what tomorrow will bring. What is your life? For you are a mist that appears for a little time and then vanishes. Instead you ought to say, "If the Lord wills, we will live and do this or that." As it is, you boast in your arrogance. All such boasting is evil. So whoever knows the right thing to do and fails to do it, for him it is sin. (Jas 4:13–17)

James warns us about the danger of failing to remember our mortality, and he confronts the person who says that she or he will travel on business to a certain town and remain for a certain period of time in order to make money—to make a profit. The words "make a profit" are significant in this passage.

> The merchants' claims are fourfold, and James put them into the future tense to give them vitality and conviction, even while he exposes the shameless, impious presumption of these people: (1) "we will go," (2) we will "spend a year," (3) we will be "doing business," and (4) we will be "making money." First, time is under their control: they will do these things "today and tomorrow." Second, location is also under their control: "we will go to such and such a town." Third, the duration of their business dealings is in their hands: "spend a year there." Fourth, their labors and profits are under their control: "doing business and making money." . . . The last term, "making money," is the goal of James's rhetoric: the merchants have it all mapped out, and the goal is financial profit.[4]

---

3. Moll, *The Art of Dying*, 13–26, 39–49; 171–79.

4. McKnight, *Letter of James*, 369–70.

The whole thrust of this attitude that James is correcting is the one that assumes that I can provide for myself in independence of God. Self-sufficiency is the problem. The problem James confronts is one that foolishly thinks that I will profit and provide for myself and for my family without consideration for God, who is my creator and the one who sustains me. Yet James asserts that a person does not really know what tomorrow will bring—not with certainty. A person's life is mist that appears for a little while and then disappears. It is like the morning ground fog that burns away with the heat of the midday sun. Instead, James affirms, a person ought to confess his or her dependence upon God. "If the Lord wills, we will live and do this or that" (Jas 4:15). This attitude indicates dependence upon one's creator, not a confident and presumptuous independence from him.[5] James states that this presumption of independence is boasting and arrogant, and this is evil (Jas 4:16). To know that one must, in trust, express one's dependence upon God and to fail to do this is sin (Jas 4:17).

This I came to see as my own sin, at least in part. I had planned for my future, virtually every step of the way, with a token acknowledgment of my dependence upon God and my own mortality. I would have said that it was more than this, but my journey through this dark valley exposed presumption that I had ignored. Now I would have said as emphatically as most who read this book that this presumption was not true and that I indeed did live in dependence upon God. But faced with the prospects of a very uncertain future, this facade of faith fell swiftly and with devastating impact on my life. What I believed during tranquil times was not so easy to swallow now that I had been diagnosed with a stage IV cancer. Plans for my future were swiftly exposed for what they were when I could no longer ignore my mortality and the fragility of my life.

It is hardly clear that James wants us to live our lives without any consideration of a plan or a purpose. It is not planning for the future that is the problem. It is the planning for the future without consideration of our dependence upon God that is the problem. Specifically, it is the planning for our provision in the future that James criticizes.

5. Moo, *Letter of James*, 204–7; and Blomberg and Kamell, *James*, 208–9. McKnight (*Letter of James*, 374–76) argues for an alternative interpretation, in which this statement continues James's rebuke of this presumption despite what these merchants are saying.

More narrowly, then, James is speaking of the merchant who knows God's providence and care, his own finitude, and his need to trust in God, but does not act on the basis of that knowledge. For such a person, that disregard of God in financial planning is sinful. James speaks of sin emerging from desire (1:15), of sin as partiality (2:9) and of sins being confessed and forgiven (5:15–16, 20). But here he envisions the sin of presumption and of knowledgeable and culpable disregard of God in business pursuits.[6]

This approach to life and to my own pursuit of provision for my family is boasting because it assumes that I can create something for myself that is independent of my relationship with my creator. It presumes that I live independently from the one who sustains my life. It assumes that I can provide for my material needs apart from God, who is my creator and the one who sustains life itself. This is arrogance because it betrays a false sense of independence. James compels us to acknowledge that it is actually sin.

Is it possible to say the words "if the Lord wills" without obedience to this Scripture? Certainly. Many of us know saints who regularly and routinely say something like this whenever the topic of future plans are discussed, and probably many (or even most) both trust this to be true and allow this to influence actual behavior. For them, this expression is not a mere cliché without content or meaning. But sometimes we may be tempted to fall into the habit of using this statement from James as a kind of "religious slogan." James is not suggesting that we merely tack on the words "if the Lord wills" to everything we say. It is important to say them, but it is equally important to trust them and to act upon them. Do my attitudes and actions reflect a belief that the Lord is ultimately in charge of my life, both in its direction and duration? Simply to say these words is not so much the question. Do I trust this and act upon this? Do I make daily decisions in light of the fact that I am a mortal creature who lives in dependence upon the Creator?

James's instruction is not unique in Scripture; the importance of a daily life lived in dependence upon God is clearly taught elsewhere in the Bible. In Proverbs, for example, we are encouraged to remember this: "Do not boast about tomorrow; for you do not know what a day may bring" (Prov 27:1). Job knows this truth well and compares the length of his life to a mere breath: "Remember that my life is a breath; my eye will never again

---

6. McKnight, *Letter of James*, 379.

see good. . . . As the cloud fades and vanishes, so he who goes down to Sheol does not come up. . . . I loathe my life; I would not live forever. Leave me alone, for my days are a breath" (Job 7:7, 9, 16). Certainly Job's recent and tragic turn of events in his life left him little choice but to confront his mortality and the brevity of life. The Psalms make this same comparison between the brevity of life and a mist or a breath:

> Behold, you have made my days a few handbreadths, and my lifetime is as nothing before you. Surely all mankind stands as a mere breath! Surely a man goes about as a shadow! Surely for nothing they are in turmoil; man heaps up wealth and does not know who will gather! (Ps 39:5–6).

The Psalms also compare a human lifetime to smoke that is blown by the wind: "For my days pass away like smoke, and my bones burn like a furnace" (Ps 102:3). A lifetime is indeed brief and temporary, according to the Psalms: "Man is like a breath; his days are like a passing shadow" (Ps 144:4). James is not alone in this basic affirmation of the brevity of life.

The song of Moses in the Psalms is focused on this theme. In sharp contrast to God's eternal nature (Ps 90:1–4), humanity is like the grass that flourishes for a while but eventually fades and withers (Ps 90:5–6). The song of Moses continues with a reminder that, in a fallen world, our lives have a limit:

> For all our days pass away under your wrath; we bring our years to an end like a sigh. The years of our life are seventy, or even by reason of strength eighty; yet their span is but toil and trouble; they are soon gone, and we fly away. (Ps 90:9–10)

The Psalmist pleads with the reader to "number our days, that we may get a heart of wisdom" (Ps 90:12).[7] Wisdom for living well in this life that has its share of toil and trouble comes from an accurate assessment and remembrance of our mortality. Such wisdom for living calls out to the Lord to return to show mercy; and it asks how much longer (Ps 90:13). Ultimately hope is in the future divine deliverance from toil and trouble, and the appropriate question this poses is—how long?

Jesus himself, of course, taught this same basic truth in a part of the Sermon on the Mount (Matt 6:25–34). In fact, it is possible that Jesus's

---

7. Spencer and Spencer, *Joy through the Night*, 38.

teaching is the source for James's instruction.[8] In his teaching on anxiety and worry about basic needs in this life, Jesus indicated that God cares for our basic provision so we are not to worry about this. If God cares for birds and flowers and provides what they need, he certainly cares for and will provide for the needs of his people. In relation specifically to the duration of life, Jesus taught in this sermon: "And which of you by being anxious can add a single hour to his span of life? . . . Therefore do not be anxious about tomorrow, for tomorrow will be anxious for itself. Sufficient for the day is its own trouble" (Matt. 6:27, 34). Anxiety and worry cannot prolong our lives by a single moment. And notice that this exhortation about worry for tomorrow does not include a promise of a trouble-free present! Today is, indeed, a day with its own trouble. Worry and anxiety are unproductive and fruitless, and every day has a sufficient amount of trouble. Today is sufficient for what? It is sufficient to allow us the opportunity to continue to trust in God who provides for birds and flowers and will surely provide what we need, even in and through times of trouble.

Scripture reminds us of the truth that we often wish to ignore, at least in our day-to-day attitudes and actions. Our brief lives in this fallen world are compared to the brevity of a mist, smoke, or the shortness of a breath. When a serious and life-threatening disease strikes us, it is impossible to ignore this truth any longer. At the age of forty-five, cancer compelled me to come face to face with my mortality. The truth about the brevity of my life to which I had paid lip service had now invaded my home—my living room, my kitchen, even my bedroom. The truth about my mortality (which I had confessed for most of my life) had suddenly and viciously become quite personal and intense. I had a wife of twenty-four years and five children: a grown son who worked full-time, a daughter in college whom we were helping to support, a son in high school, a ten-year-old son, and a nine-year-old daughter. What would happen to them, if I died? What would happen to all that I had hoped and planned to see and to do in our family life?

I had indeed lived my life with many assumptions about my family. Yes, I knew that I was a mortal and that tomorrow was not promised to me. This I would have confessed with my lips. But I pretty much lived daily life oblivious to this. I assumed, almost as my right, many typical experiences with my family. For example, I assumed that one day I would

8. Moo, *Letter of James*, 204.

walk my daughters down the aisle on their wedding days. Actually, from the day both of our daughters were born and often throughout their lives, I thought of their wedding days. The role of father of the bride was a joy and privilege that I refused to relinquish! I also assumed the pleasure of getting to know my sons as they matured. I looked forward to the delight that comes to a dad who watches his sons pursue a life's work and the things that interest them. I very much wanted to see how they would use well their gifts in life. Perhaps most importantly, I assumed that I would live to a ripe old age with my wife. I anticipated a long life with her. We sometimes discussed plans to grow old together and sit in rocking chairs on our porch. I very much anticipated many, many years together. I looked forward to sharing our role as grandparents with her, and we had discussed some of the travel we wanted to do as we approached and entered retirement age. I delighted in the prospects for all our experiences together for decades to come. I very much looked forward to all of this with my family, and so much more!

I looked forward to the opportunity to provide for my family. I have never been wealthy, nor have I aspired to great wealth in this life. The pursuit of money and wealth has never been a priority. I have never been in a position to provide much more than the basics for my family, but I assumed that I would be around to do this for many, many years. This was more than an assumption for me, though. This was more of an expectation, a right that I claimed for myself. What could be more right than for me to assume than that I would need to be here to provide for my family? I very much wanted to be around to pay the mortgage and to provide food and clothing for my wife and children. This was my expectation, and it was even my right!

But the diagnosis of cancer shattered this assumption for me. It devastated this expectation. All that I had assumed about my future with my family seemed to be snatched away in a moment. And as the months of chemotherapy ground on and on, this only seemed to confirm that my life would be short—at least short from the perspective of where I stood then! My oldest daughter, for example, was beginning her sophomore year at Gordon College, and it did not seem very certain at all that I would be around to watch her graduate in a mere three years' time. Perhaps, but it was not certain. It looked even less likely that I would see her wedding day. Does this sound familiar? Does this not sound like James's instruction? I had assumed that I would certainly be around for these times, and many more than these. But cancer and its debilitating treatment had brought me to a place where I must pay more than lip service to the truth—the truth that my life is like a vapor that blows away with the slightest breeze. My life is a mist that quickly burns away with the heat of the midday sun.

We are not here forever. Our lives are compared to a mist that is soon gone. I have lived in New England for many years and in England for a brief time during my study at Durham University. Both are places where the fog can be very persistent. Sometimes the mist burns it away in a few hours, and other times it seems to hang around in the air longer than expected. But sooner or later, the bright sunshine burns it away, and it is gone. James says that our lives are like this, despite what we tell ourselves. Our lives are brief, and we do not really know what tomorrow holds for us. In a similar way, Scripture also compares our lives to smoke that a breeze can easily blow away and to a breath, which is very short indeed! We are mortal, and our lives are brief.

Jonathan Edwards is one of the important people connected with the First Great Awakening in America. His life and work have undoubtedly left a significant impact on the history of Christ's church in North America, an impact that continues for some to this day.[9] Edwards famously wrote a series of resolutions for his life, which he reportedly read weekly. There are seventy resolutions in this list, and it was completed on August 17, 1723, when Edwards was about twenty years old.[10] Several of these resolutions embody the biblical truth we have considered. Edwards plainly intended to live his life with his mortality in view: "Many of these resolutions are directed toward trying never to lose focus on spiritual things. In a number of them, he reminded himself, as he had been taught since childhood, to think of his own dying, or to live as though he had only an hour left before his death or 'before I should hear the last trump.'"[11] Six of these seventy resolutions are explicitly focused on this very topic:

- Resolved, to live with all my might, while I do live. (6)

- Resolved, never to do anything, which I should be afraid to do, if it were the last hour of my life. (7)

9. Marsden, *Jonathan Edwards*; Piper, *God's Passion for His Glory: Living the Vision of Jonathan Edwards*; and Piper and Taylor, *A God-Entranced Vision of All Things*.

10 Edwards, "The Resolutions of Jonathan Edwards" [1722–1723], http://www.jonathan-edwards.org/Resolutions.html.

11. Marsden, *Jonathan Edwards*, 50–51.

- Resolved, to think much on all occasions of my own dying, and of the common circumstances which attend death. (9)

- Resolved, that I will live so as I shall wish I had done when I come to die. (17)

- Resolved, to live so at all times, as I think is best in my devout frames, and when I have clearest notions of things of the gospel, and another world. (18)

- Resolved, never to do anything, which I should be afraid to do, if I expected it would not be above an hour, before I should hear the last trump. (19)

Jonathan Edwards clearly intended to live his life with its end in view. He purposed to live fully aware that a person is not here forever, and he expressly lived as though each day might be his last day.

Some of us, perhaps, find this perspective on life to be difficult, or even impossible.[12] I confess that I certainly did before my illness. Yes, I professed then that I am mortal and the life I have on this earth is brief. And, yes, I would confess then that my life is in God's hands and that I live in dependence upon him. But my daily actions and activities told a different story. However, when a person is assaulted by a stage IV cancer, this compels one to stare deeply into the face of one's own mortality and the brevity of one's life. Frankly, this news from my doctor came to me like a death sentence. When I was first diagnosed, my doctor had emphasized to me that, in the early stages, my particular kind of cancer had a very high success rate with a well-established treatment that had proven quite effective for several decades. And then several tests, including a bone marrow biopsy, were done to stage my cancer—to see how far advanced it was in my body. Stage I is the earliest and stage IV is very advanced. When the doctor shared this news with me, that my cancer was in a very advanced state, he then said that he was "still hopeful" that the treatment might prove effective in putting this cancer into remission. The tone in his voice left me unsure about the level of his own confidence in this, however. It very much sounded to me that the three or four decades of life that I had assumed were in my future were being cut considerably short. I had been caught in my presumption about my life and my plans for it.

12. Moll, *The Art of Dying*, 9–11.

I would like to be able to say that I am a changed man and that my attitude and actions are completely in line with James's exhortation. However, I can bear witness to how easily we can slip back into comfortable patterns of life, especially in our largely insulated and comfortable Western world. Yes, I am a different person in some very significant ways since my cancer has been in remission. Indeed, I bear some physical symptoms that remind me daily of this horrible experience. I cannot escape some physical reminders of this time of trouble for me and my family, even if I tried. Yet I also have been surprised, and a bit discouraged, frankly, at how easily I have slid back into the very attitude at which James takes direct aim. It is all too easy to presume on the future and plan for it as though my future is completely in my control. It is easy to forget James's lesson, even when it is learned through the crucible of suffering.

We would do well to live our lives more often in light of our mortality and the brevity of life. In our culture this is often perceived as morbid, but it does not necessarily need to be. Certainly a fixation on the brevity of life and our own mortality can paralyze us, and this is not what I am suggesting here. But we are creatures who live in a fallen world in which death reigns over us now, and sooner or later, if the Lord does not return, we all face the end of our lives here on this earth. Rob Moll has recently encouraged Christians to recover what previous generations of believers have known and practiced with respect to our mortality and the fragility of life. He writes,

> Dying is an art only because through it God is at work. Only in God's hand can something ugly and terrible be transformed into a thing of beauty and purpose. In the end death is as mysterious to us as resurrection. . . . we must practice for our deaths, prepare to care for others as they face it and look for the hand of God who welcomes us through death to life everlasting.[13]

A life that is lived with its end in view may indeed yield the fruit of a life that is lived well.

We often simply choose to ignore this reality that we are mortal human beings who live in a fallen world. In our fairly comfortable Western world we more easily allow ourselves to be deceived in the course of daily living. It is only when serious illness or some other catastrophic

13. Ibid., 178–79.

circumstance assaults our sense of safety and security that we can no longer ignore the fragility of our lives. The death of a family member or a close friend reminds us that we are not here on this earth forever. And when we ignore our own mortality and the brevity of our lives, we are in danger of presumption—the presumption that we live independently of our Creator. This is the sin that James seeks to challenge and correct. If we chose, instead, to live more and more with a recognition of James's teaching that we are a mist—here today and gone tomorrow—we may find that we have more purpose to our days. We may discover what it means to live more and more in dependence upon our Creator who sustains us and holds our lives in his hands.

> *October 10, 2005*
>
> *Don't take him away from us. Your word says to pray "not my will but yours," but I am having a hard time not being selfish. I keep thinking, "I love him so much, and I'm not done being married to him." We hope and pray for the best to happen soon, but what if it really is your will to take him? All our days are numbered. Are Jeff's days to be shorter than his parents'? Lord, I can't stand this. Some days I feel like I'm going to crack! I'm so selfish, and then I feel guilty for that sin. I want to be strong, but some days I'm like a lost three-year-old child. I'm scared, lonely, sad, striving for a normal sense of living, and unsure of the future. Oh, God! I'm hurting—and if I am, how does Jeff feel inside? Sometimes when he gets in the mood to talk, he gets emotional and teary. My strong husband is being beaten up emotionally, spiritually, and physically. Please, God, take this away from him. Let me be the one with it! I said that on the day of his surgery. I still feel that way. I guess I'm feeling down and confused today. I'm sorry, Lord! I need sleep; tomorrow is a very early morning. Thank you, God, for listening! Good night!*

6

Financial Fear

When I am afraid, I put my trust in you. In God, whose word I praise, in God I trust; I shall not be afraid. What can flesh do to me?

—Psalm 56:3–4

August 7, 2005

If God takes my love, how will we survive? Besides the incredible hole in our lives, I can't make enough money to pay all the bills. I'll lose our physical shelter. I'll need to get more work, lots more work. How will I raise the kids the way Jeff and I want them to be raised if I have to work two or three jobs? I know this sounds very selfish, but as a mom I have to think of the kids and their future. If it was just me, I wouldn't mind working around the clock. I could get a tiny apartment with no yard. But if I had to sell the house to pay all the bills, I may not be in any better situation because to rent a place big enough for us would cost the same as our mortgage. Trying to think that through is not pleasant. But I don't think I want to continue to live if I can't live with Jeff at my side. I'm so selfish. I want Jeff. I don't want to let God have him.

October 11, 2005

God, what are your plans for Jeff? Do you plan to heal him? I feel like I'm losing him one day at a time! He can't stay out of bed for one hour without great effort! Walking is so tiresome. He can't read books anymore. It takes all he has to work on prepping for class. Are you taking him now, slowly? Please don't, Lord! Please heal my mate! Please, God!

October 28, 2005

One of the classes at Oak Hills is planning a benefit dinner for Jeff this Saturday. It's a class project. So far we haven't needed a lot of extra for medical expenses. I don't know what's down the road. Maybe he will need a blood transfusion or worse a bone marrow transplant. Those things may not be covered by insurance, and God may be planning ahead for us. And we are only receiving bills from August now. But I really feel uncomfortable with people giving us so much money. So I've prayed that God will only allow enough money to be given to cover the medical needs and no more. If we don't need any money, then I pray none is raised. But only God knows the future.

To say that cancer produces concern in a person would be, without a doubt, a gross understatement. Fear is the more appropriate word. Many Christians I know, though, seem to want to do whatever it takes to avoid the use of the word *fear* for any experience that a believer may face. Before my illness, I would have counted myself among these Christians. I am not sure anymore that this is very helpful or even in touch with reality. The regular encouragement in Scripture in the face of troubling times suggests that fear is a normal, or at least a regular, response to the shock of the experience of challenge, trouble, and suffering in this life. Fear is a frequent, natural response of fallen people who live in a fallen world that sometimes assaults us with suffering.

Scripture frequently seems to assume that this tendency to fear is a regular and natural response to suffering and trouble, and it often confronts this tendency with an encouragement to people who face fearsome circumstances in life. This encouragement can be stated either negatively ("do not be afraid" or "do not fear") or positively (often with language such as "be strong and courageous"). For example, Deuteronomy records Moses's encouragement to the Israelites as they consider their entrance into the Promised Land. The previous generation had faltered and failed to trust the Lord's protection and provision as they considered the fearsome opponents and obstacles in the land (Num 13–14).[1] As Moses recounts this failure to trust the Lord, he encourages the current generation of Israelites to trust him. Moses comments specifically on that previous generation's rebellion in the wilderness, and he commands the Israelites who are to enter the land: "Do not fear or be dismayed" (Deut 1:21) and "Do not be in dread or afraid of them" (Deut 1:29). These pairs of verbs in verses 21 and 29 occur commonly together in Scripture, and they together function to indicate a confidence in the Lord and his ability to deliver from danger.[2] Moses's command to this generation is

1. von Rad, *Deuteronomy*, 40–41.
2. Merrill, *Deuteronomy*, 73.

clear, but at the same time fear is real and must be confronted.[3] This is the point of the commands!

Appropriately enough, after Moses's death and as Joshua is preparing to lead the Israelites across the Jordan River and into the Promised Land, he himself also receives this same encouragement, stated positively here: be strong and courageous (Josh 1:6–7, 9, 18). Joshua is the new leader of the nation of Israel, and he is commissioned with the task that the previous generation had failed to accomplish, despite the fact that Moses himself was their leader. This commission for Joshua is a reaffirmation of his role after Moses's death, as is clear when the language of Joshua 1 is compared with Moses's words to Joshua at the end of Deuteronomy (Deut 31:7).[4] Joshua's encouragement comes both from the Lord himself (Josh 1:6–7, 9) and from the people of Israel (Josh 1:18). This command to be courageous and strong in the face of a fearsome circumstance is grounded in the affirmation of the Lord's presence: "No man shall be able to stand before you all the days of your life. Just as I was with Moses, so I will be with you" (Josh 1:5); "Do not be frightened, and do not be dismayed, for the Lord your God is with you wherever you go" (Josh 1:9); and "Only may the Lord your God be with you, as he was with Moses!" (Josh 1:17). Joshua's strength and courage to stand well in a fearsome situation and against any and all opponents is rooted in the reminder of the Lord's presence with him.[5] The literary structure of this part of the narrative (Josh 1:6–9) begins and ends with the same command to be strong and courageous, and it indicates that this command is the main theme of this divine speech to Joshua.[6]

The encouragement from Moses to the Israelites, and the same encouragement from the Lord to Joshua, continues as a constant thread through Scripture.[7] This encouragement (not to fear and to be strong and courageous) is an acknowledgement of the natural tendency in a fallen world to fear what threatens our safety and security. It is a normal

---

3. Brueggemann, *Deuteronomy*, 29–31; and Merrill, *Deuteronomy*, 79.

4. McConville and Williams, *Joshua*, 13–14.

5. Hubbard, *Joshua*, 79–81; and Gangel, *Joshua*, 13.

6. Hubbard, *Joshua*, 79. Specifically, this literary structure is an inclusio.

7. For example, stated negatively ("do not be afraid") Deut 20:1, 3; 2 Kgs 25:24; Ps 46:2; 91:5; Isa 10:24; 35:4; Jer 1:8; Matt 10:28, 31; John 14:27; and Heb 13:6; and stated positively ("be strong and/or be courageous") Deut 31:6–7, 23; Josh 10:25; 2 Sam 7:27; 1 Chr 22:13; 28:20; 2 Chr 19:11; 32:7; Matt 14:27; Mark 6:50; Acts 23:11; 27:22, 25; 1 Cor 16:13; Phil 1:20; and Heb 3:6.

and natural response for fallen people who live in a fallen world—even for people of faith. This is not to say that fear should be left unchecked or unchallenged (this is precisely the point of these commands!), but it is merely to acknowledge that it is a regular and very real part of the experience of suffering in a fallen world. The trouble of life often leads to the companionship of fear through these days of trouble.

I will freely admit that fear was my companion on the pathway of suffering through cancer and its treatment. This does not mean that it consumed me or caused me completely to lose sight of God's presence with me and his promises to me. But it is simply true. It is reality that I experienced fear, almost daily, when I was ill. I say "almost" because it is possible that my memory of this experience is faulty enough to have forgotten a day or two when this was not a reality for me. But my memory is that fear was a regular companion as I walked through this valley. Fear stalked my every step through this dark and seemingly endless valley. It followed me into each exam and treatment room. It lingered around virtually every conversation. It greeted me each morning; it snuggled up against me as I fell asleep.

As a husband and a father with a young family, one of my first and very pressing concerns was the financial impact of this disease and its treatment. After the initial shock began to subside, the financial impact upon our family's modest budget began to weigh upon my thoughts more and more heavily. How would we pay for the very expensive treatment? Where would the financial support come from if I could not work? Perhaps here again was evidence of the presumption that James's instruction had exposed in me. Perhaps it exposed my presumption that I was really living my life in some measure in independence from God; I really provided for myself and for my family. And if I were no longer here to provide, how would the needs of my wife and my children be met?

Fear quickly leads to worry. The two go together naturally. Yet Scripture regularly encourages us, and even commands us, not to worry or be anxious in times of trouble. Jesus, in the Sermon on the Mount, instructs us that we cannot add an hour to our lives through worry because the God who provides for birds and flowers surely will provide for us.

> But if God so clothes the grass of the field, which today is alive and tomorrow is thrown into the oven, will he not much more clothe you, O you of little faith? Therefore do not be anxious, saying, "What shall we eat?" or "What shall we drink?" or "What

shall we wear?" For the Gentiles seek after all these things, and your heavenly Father knows that you need them all. But seek first the kingdom of God and his righteousness, and all these things will be added to you. (Matt 6:30–33)

God knows our situation and knows our need, whatever we face. Life is about more than food and clothing (Matt 6:25), but God knows what we need and will provide according to his priorities and plan: "Jesus, who regards God's original creation purpose as still valid (Mt 19:4–6), believes that the God who cares for unemployed animals will care still more for his children, regardless of their economic situation."[8] So Jesus commands us not to be anxious about the most basic of our needs—food and clothing.[9]

I do not find in Scripture that this encouragement to refrain from fear and anxiety is to be a stoic—to deny the reality of pain and suffering. Scripture does not expect us to ignore or deny the reality of the pain we experience. It does not assume we will simply bear up all on our own. Instead, Scripture regularly encourages us to use trouble and suffering, along with the sense of need exposed by these times, to turn to God and to trust in him: "When I am afraid, I put my trust in you. In God, whose word I praise, in God I trust; I shall not be afraid. What can flesh do to me?" (Ps 56:3–4). Psalm 56 holds together fear and trust. The subjective experience of fear may persist, but in these situations trust is anchored on God and his promises. Trust in God may not remove the fearsome circumstances, but it makes it possible to live even when fear is the natural response for people who live in a fallen world.[10] When fear comes during a time of trouble and suffering, as it inevitably will, put your trust in God because he cares for you.

This encouragement to turn to the Lord and trust him when we are assaulted by fear and anxiety occurs often in the Bible: "Humble yourselves, therefore, under the mighty hand of God so that at the proper time he may exalt you, casting all your anxieties on him, because he cares for you" (1 Pet 5:6–7). Scripture encourages a humble submission as a creature under the mighty hand of one's creator. It commends trust in God as the antidote to anxiety: "The Lord is my light and my salvation; whom shall I fear? The Lord is the stronghold of my life; of whom

8. Keener, *Matthew*, 154.
9. Blomberg, *Matthew*, 125–27; and Keener, *Matthew*, 155.
10. Goldingay, *Psalms*, 2:185.

shall I be afraid?" (Ps 27:1. "Behold, God is my salvation; I will trust, and will not be afraid; for the Lord God is my strength and my song, and he has become my salvation" (Isa 12:2). Trust in God who is our salvation and the one who delivers from the fearful situation that assaults us.

Does this mean that God has promised to deliver us now from suffering? Not necessarily; but he may choose to do so, as God delivered Paul from what he considered a certain death (2 Cor 1:8–11).[11] Trust in God in times of trouble does not necessarily guarantee deliverance now from the trouble that leads to anxiety. And anxiety may continue to bark at our heels through times of suffering, but it need not devour us when we cast our cares upon the one who is our salvation and the one who cares for us. Paul even went so far as to command rejoicing in everything, even suffering:

> Rejoice in the Lord always; again I will say, Rejoice. Let your reasonableness be known to everyone. The Lord is at hand; do not be anxious about anything, but in everything by prayer and supplication with thanksgiving let your requests be made known to God. And the peace of God, which surpasses all understanding will guard your hearts and your minds in Christ Jesus. (Phil. 4:4–7)

Paul is no ivory-tower theologian who is detached from real life and its suffering. His own letters recount many instances of suffering in his ministry as an apostle of Jesus Christ. As we bring everything to the Lord in prayer and supplication with thanksgiving, God's peace will guard our hearts and our minds in Christ Jesus in all of life, including suffering.

The suffering may still exist, along with its pain and the concern that so easily springs from it. The word translated "will guard" in Philippians 4:7 has the connotation of a garrison that guards and protects a city from the hostility and danger that lurks outside the city walls.[12] In the world in which Paul lived, cities were regularly surrounded by a wall that was meant for protection, especially at night. This wall guarded the residents from the danger outside its walls. The danger still existed there, but the wall and the garrison that patrolled its walls would provide a sense of safety and security for those who trusted the strength of those walls (and also the garrison to do their work well!). This wall that guarded the city

---

11. See chapter 3 for more discussion on this situation that Paul faced.

12. Fee, *Paul's Letter to the Philippians*, 411; Hansen, *Letter to the Philippians*, 294; and Thielman, *Philippians*, 219.

protected those who remained within it! Peace was provided for those who trusted it to protect from the danger that was still there outside the walls. Prayer to the God who is present with us even in suffering can produce peace in us. God's presence produces a peace for those who trust him enough to come before him in prayer.

X   I have never considered myself to be the kind of person who worried about money and finances too much. I would have considered myself a person who trusted in God for his material needs both for today and for the future. For example, our family had lived in England for a year as I began a post-graduate degree at a university there, and I could not work during that year because I was an international student who entered the country on a student visa. Our financial support for this academic year involved several scholarships, some personal savings, and some support from family. At the end of this year and after carefully budgeting during our time in England, most of this support had been spent. Without a job to at least supplement this support, we lived entirely on a "fixed income" for nine months. As a result, when we returned from our time at the university in England I had no job, no house or apartment, no car, no credit card, and a very, very small amount of cash in my pocket. Despite hardships and some anxious moments, I had seen God provide what we needed in some extreme circumstances, and I had grown to trust him more and more through these experiences.

I thought that I had learned this lesson well, but apparently not so well. One of the first thoughts that I had when I got past the initial shock of this diagnosis was this very question: Who would provide for the needs of my family when I was gone? I had pursued theological and pastoral training in response to a sense of God's calling on my life, and I had served mostly in a small church and small Christian college context. Financial security had not been a high priority in my life. And without either personal or employer-provided life insurance in which to trust my family's future, anxiety and fear began to seep into my mind and my heart. Our oldest daughter was in her sophomore year at a private Christian college. Our three youngest children lived at home and were in middle school and elementary school. My wife worked, but part-time. I wanted very much to be here to provide for them, but this was now very much in doubt. Who would provide for my family if I were unable to work or if I died?

In addition to this concern, I had the issue of the cost of the treatment for my cancer to consider. Since I had moved from a pastoral position in a church that had paid fully for our health insurance to a new position at a small Christian college, our health coverage had changed. It was far from certain to what extent this new health insurance would pay for the significant cost of the medical bills for my treatment. Our former coverage had been very good, but we heard whispers and rumors that our new coverage might not cover as much. I had a series of tests to diagnose and to stage this cancer. There were regular appointments with my oncologist and for treatment. A consultation with a leading expert on Lymphoma and Hodgkin's Lymphoma at the University of Minnesota required a trip to see him in September. I had regular chemotherapy that involved four specific drugs, with a fifth drug—a newer and very expensive drug—added to the mix after four months of treatment. Each chemotherapy treatment cost an average of four thousand dollars, with the addition of this newer drug Rituximub (also known as Rituxan) adding more than sixty-eight hundred dollars to the cost of each treatment. How would we pay for all of these expensive appointments, tests, and treatments?

God had some lessons to teach me. I would have another opportunity to learn to trust him even more. When I heard the diagnosis, which at the time sounded like a death sentence to me, I naturally became anxious for my family's provision. What if I could not work very much, or at all, for a prolonged period of time? What if I died? Anxiety and fear flooded into my mind and my heart. At first, I found it almost impossible to hold back this anxiety and fear.

As I looked forward to a very uncertain future at the beginning of the 2005 academic year at Oak Hills Christian College, I could only see disaster on the horizon. Actually, the year that I was in treatment was, by far, the most financially stable year of our marriage. And I do mean "by far." Chris and I have now been married for thirty years, and God has always provided for our needs. But in a life pursued in response to a call to ministry, our family finances have often been fairly tight. When I was a pastor, one of the members of the church I served said to me once, "Pastor Jeff, I know what we pay you. . . . Chris must be a magician!" I assured her that there was no magic involved, at least on my wife's part or mine. We have never had very much that would naturally inspire financial security for the future, but God has always provided. I thought that I knew how to trust God for our financial needs when times were tough and finances tight.

But apparently God had something more to teach me. During this year of illness, when everything—financially at least—would be expected to come apart at the seams, God provided for us most abundantly. And very often God provided for us through his people. Many, many people sent cards of encouragement, and many included a gift to help with medical expenses. My family regularly sent generous gifts to help us with some of our basic household needs. Our health insurance paid for much more of the share of the cost of treatment than we had been expecting. My employer kept me on full-time for this academic year, even though I was not able to work anything close to full time. This was a significant and sacrificial commitment for a very small, independent college. I am not sure everyone actually supported this decision, because I am not sure that I really did either! But the administrative leadership made clear to me their commitment to stand with my family during this trial, and I am thankful for this.

It is very clear that this year when I was ill was by far the most financially stable year of our marriage. Two further examples of the generosity of God's people helped to make this so. A freshman class at the college had been in the practice of doing a service project each year. This service project typically involved fundraising to help meet a need, or it involved the investment of time to help meet a need in the community—or both. Early in the fall semester one of the students in that class approached me about their service project for that year; they had decided that they wanted to help raise funds for our family's needs during this illness. Among other things they did that fall, they sponsored a dinner hosted at the church we attended that raised about eight thousand dollars to help us. Their concern and generosity expressed toward us was overwhelming. A photograph of this class with my wife and me is framed and sits on a shelf that overlooks the computer where I write this. It is a regular reminder of their love expressed to us and of God's provision for our need.

Another example of a very sacrificial gift given to help meet our need came from a member of a church that I had served previously. This person called my wife while I was ill and told her that a card was in the mail with a gift for us and that we needed to keep it. We could not send it back! This woman was a single mom who was herself working her way through college and was raising two daughters. She certainly could have looked to provide for her own needs with this money, and no one could have faulted her. She surely did not have much "extra" in her budget. and even if she did, she could have used what she sent to help provide for her own family. But she told my wife that she had recently received a small inheritance from her mom who had died of cancer, and she wanted to send a gift of part of this money to help us. Soon after this phone conversation, a card came in the mail with a check for three thousand dollars. God used her generosity to provide for us when circumstances for our family looked very grim; he had used her generosity to encourage our hearts and our minds in Christ Jesus.

I had thought that finances were not a concern for me, but through this valley I learned that they were—much more than I had thought. I found myself very much anxious for our financial future, whether I lived or I died from this disease. But God met our needs in many unexpected ways. In addition to the very sacrificial gifts of so many people, our health insurance fully paid almost all of the costs of my treatment. I came to realize that what looked to be very unclear and uncertain at the beginning of this treatment actually turned out to be a better health insurance coverage than we had previously in pastoral ministry. Thus, another cause of concern, anxiety, and even fear was met with God's gracious hand of provision. In many ways, that year of illness was the most financially stable year of our marriage, even though nothing about this would have been expected from a human perspective. But God taught me in new and fresh ways that, even in my suffering and pain, he was with me, and he would care for my family, whatever came my way.

The book of Hebrews encourages the readers to continue in perseverance in faith. They are facing a variety of challenges to their faith, including persecution and financial loss (Heb 10:32–34). They even accepted the loss of property with joy because they trusted in God's promises for the future: "and you joyfully accepted the plundering of your property, since you knew that you yourselves had a better possession and an abiding one" (Heb 10:34). These promises for the future are detailed in the great "Hall of Faith" in Hebrews 11, where many who trusted God did not allow anything that this life threw at them, the good or the bad, to distract them from trust in God and in his promises for the future. God sometimes delivers from pain and suffering experienced now in a fallen world; he will deliver from suffering in the promised new heaven and new earth, the New Creation (Heb 12:25–29). In Hebrews' final encouragement to perseverance in faith, we read:

> Keep your life free from love of money, and be content with what you have, for he has said, "I will never leave you nor forsake you." So we can confidently say, "The Lord is my helper; I will not fear; what can man do to me?" (Heb 13:5–6)

Hebrews commands a trust in the Lord who helps, protects, and provides.[13] Yet central to Hebrews' message is the necessity of perseverance despite the apparent delay in God's fulfillment of his promises. Even a superficial reading of the great "Hall of Faith" (Heb 11) indicates that those who are commended for faith died before they saw God's promises fulfilled; yet they persevered in faith throughout their lifetimes with a faith that constantly looked forward in hope to the fulfillment of his promises. Death itself did not dissuade them from trust in God's presence and his promises. Thus Hebrews commands a trust in the Lord who is present and who has promised a sure and certain inheritance in the kingdom of God.[14] What is the antidote to the poison of fear and anxiety that so easily infects us? What is the secret to dealing with fear when financial disaster looms over us? We must continue to walk in perseverance. We must continue to trust in God who is with us and to trust in his promises to us. Indeed, what can mere people and circumstance do to us?

> *November 21, 2005*
> *We received a check for $8007.00. Pam told me that the money could be spent for whatever we need to spend it on. We could use it for plane fare for Megs, car repairs, food, heat, or medical costs. We could spend it on whatever our family needs happen to be. I felt so much better after she said this.*

---

13. Hagner, *Encountering the Book of Hebrews*, 171.

14. Johnson, *Hebrews*, 343–44.

7

Encouragement from God's People

Blessed be the God and Father of our Lord Jesus Christ, the Father of mercies and God of all comfort, who comforts us in all our affliction, so that we may be able to comfort those who are in any affliction, with the comfort with which we ourselves are comforted by God.

—2 CORINTHIANS 1:3–4

December 7, 2005

Pearl Harbor Day. Another horrible day in history. Today we got a call that Jeff's red blood cell count is too low. Tomorrow he will have a transfusion. He's very nervous. I am, too. But he's the patient, and he has to go through it. So many things can go wrong. I still wish this was me and not him.

"And please, God! Keep this from our children! May they never need to experience transfusions, countless needle pricks and chemo!"

Jeff fell Monday night. It's very icy out now, but it wasn't ice that pulled the carpet out from under his feet. It was weakness in his legs and gravity. I don't want to be away from home if he needs to go outside. If I'm home, he won't need to go out alone! Things are getting harder for him. It's harder to teach and even walk. I'm afraid for him to cook some days. What if he falls in the shower? Chemo is coming again. They've lessened one of his anti-nausea drugs since it may be the culprit for his leg weakness. So now he's very queasy after chemo. Food is gross, and taking pills makes him gag.

Yesterday was retest day! The oncologist ordered an M.R.I. to see if there was a pinched nerve or other problem to explain leg weakness, but it showed nothing unusual—just a couple of bulging discs. He also had a C.T. scan and the horrid bone marrow biopsy. We'll get the results the week of Christmas! I want my husband back!

The Apostle Paul knew suffering. In his second letter to the Corinthians, he described a so-called thorn in the flesh that had been given to him, presumably by God, to keep him from boasting in his experiences in Christ or becoming conceited in his place as the apostle to the Gentiles (2 Cor 12:1–7). At the end of 2 Corinthians 11, Paul boasted about his weakness and the suffering that showed exactly how weak he was as a human being and, by implication, how dependent upon God he really was. In 2 Corinthians 12, he continued with this boasting in his weakness when he mentioned the thorn in the flesh that God had given him to keep him humble as an apostle of Jesus Christ and as one who had extraordinary visionary experiences of heaven.[1] Paul was not specific at all about what this "thorn in the flesh" was, and the guesses over the years have been many. My best guess is that Paul is referring to some personal illness that he had for about fourteen years.[2] I think that Paul was not very specific about the exact nature of this thorn in the flesh because the important thing—for him to report to the Corinthians and for them to know about him—was not what the thorn was, but what it produced in his life. It produced an ongoing dependence upon God.

Paul described this thorn in the flesh, whatever it was, as "weakness" and that which "harasses." Paul pleaded and prayed three times for this weakness and harassment to be removed from him, but he was denied (2 Cor 12:8). God refused to remove the source of this suffering from Paul because apparently he needed to learn in this circumstance that God's grace was sufficient for him because God's power is made perfect in his weakness (2 Cor 12:9).

> Therefore I will boast all the more gladly of my weaknesses, so that the power of Christ may rest upon me. For the sake of Christ, then, I am content with weaknesses, insults, hardships, persecutions, and calamities. For when I am weak, then I am strong. (2 Cor 12:9b–10)

Through his suffering in this circumstance, Paul learned lessons about Christ's power in his life and its sufficiency for everything he faced. Paul discovered that there was strength in weakness because God's grace sustained him and met his need in his time of weakness. In his suffering, Paul did not simply try to change his attitude about his circumstances

1. Scott, *2 Corinthians*, 227.
2. Hafemann, *2 Corinthians*, 462–63.

nor did he attempt to "gut it out" in a Stoic-like mastery of mind over matter. Instead, in his suffering, Paul prayed, and this demonstrated his trust in God to deliver and to sustain.

> In stark contrast, when Paul boasts in his weakness, he is not engaging either in the self-mastery of the ancient Stoic or in the reinterpretation of events that is common to the modern "power of positive thinking" movement. For Paul, weakness is not the result of failing to control our passions or being unable to fight negative thoughts or influences. Weakness for Paul is real suffering and powerlessness because of our existence under the real power and circumstances of sin. The Self cannot subdue sin on its own. Weaknesses cannot be escaped simply by thinking differently. What is needed is not more willpower, but the power of God's grace. When confronted with his thorn in the flesh, Paul does not try to think positively; he prays. His contentment does not come from a renewed ability to exercise his will but from receiving God's grace. He is not seeking a higher virtue of contentment but a supernatural act of deliverance.[3]

In his weakness, Paul prayed. The answer to his prayer was "no," and this answer was intended to demonstrate through Paul's own life the power of God to sustain through suffering. In his weakness, Christ's power shone through more brightly.[4]

In the previous chapter in this letter to the Corinthians, Paul listed a number of different kinds of suffering that he experienced as an apostle. In contrast to false teachers who had opposed Paul and his ministry and who had boasted in their human accomplishments, Paul instead pointed to the suffering and pain he had endured in his Christian ministry.[5] The number and severity of the kinds of suffering and pain he went through is staggering.

> Are they servants of Christ? I am a better one—I am talking like a madman—with far greater labors, far more imprisonments, with countless beatings, and often near death. Five times I received at the hands of the Jews the forty lashes less one. Three times I was beaten with rods. Once I was stoned. Three times I was shipwrecked; a night and a day I was adrift at sea; on frequent journeys, in danger from rivers, danger from robbers, danger from

3. Ibid., 472.
4. Ibid., 465; and Scott, *2 Corinthians*, 230.
5. Hafemann, *2 Corinthians*, 439–41; and Scott, *2 Corinthians*, 215–19.

my own people, danger from Gentiles, danger in the city, danger in the wilderness, danger at sea, danger from false brothers; in toil and hardship, through many a sleepless night, in hunger and thirst, often without food, in cold and exposure. And, apart from other things, there is the daily pressure on me of my anxiety for all the churches. (2 Cor 11:23–28)

This list of Paul's suffering is not merely a catalogue of things that happened to Paul (as though he were just a really unlucky fellow!), but rather it is a description of the extent to which he willingly endured suffering for the sake of his apostolic ministry. He willingly endured suffering as the apostle of the crucified Christ and as one who identified in weakness with those he was called to serve, including the Corinthians themselves.[6] Paul concludes again that he "boasts" not in anything that would glorify him but rather in his weakness and suffering because, as 2 Corinthians 12 makes clear, this displays the power of Christ in him.

In the beginning of this letter Paul also described a time when he thought that he was certainly about to die (2 Cor 1:8–11). While he was in the Roman province of Asia, he was so utterly burdened beyond his strength that he despaired of life itself (2 Cor 1:8). We do not know exactly what this circumstance was, but Paul thought a death sentence had been pronounced on him; he thought his death was imminent and certain.[7]

> Paul further describes how he felt during the mortal danger described in verse 8. By stating twice in rapid succession that he thought he was going to die, Paul conveys the intensity of the situation. In fact, Paul had already pronounced a sentence of death (or "verdict of death") on himself, accepting his imminent demise as the providence of God. . . . He saw in the situation the divine purpose that he should trust solely in the God who raises the dead and not in himself.[8]

God delivered Paul to teach him to rely not on himself, but on God who raises the dead (2 Cor 1:9), and God also delivered him to give others who prayed for him the opportunity to give thanks to God (2 Cor 1:11). Paul's confidence in God's character and his promises was so strong that even death itself could not call him or his promises into

---

6. Hafemann, *2 Corinthians*, 440.

7. Ibid., 64.

8. Scott, *2 Corinthians*, 28–29.

question. God was faithful to his promise and would deliver Paul, even if he died! And his suffering and God's deliverance was also the occasion for thanksgiving to God. In and through this experience, Paul learned some lessons about God and his faithfulness, and other Christians also grew in their faith.

So Paul certainly knew suffering. In 2 Corinthians, in particular, he often describes his suffering as an apostle of Jesus Christ. Paul knew a depth and breadth of suffering in the extreme. When he wrote about the endurance of suffering, he never wrote as an ivory-tower theologian who was detached from the real world and its pain and suffering. Instead, he suffered more than most humans do, both in terms of duration and severity. He certainly suffered more than I have; this I willingly (and even gladly!) concede to him. When he began this second letter to the Corinthians with words about the source of comfort for those who suffer, he was not writing merely on the theoretical level; he knew the power of encouragement for and to those who suffer.

> Blessed be the God and Father of our Lord Jesus Christ, the Father of mercies and God of all comfort, who comforts us in all our affliction, so that we may be able to comfort those who are in any affliction, with the comfort with which we ourselves are comforted by God. (2 Cor 1:3–4)

God is to be praised because he is the God of mercy and of all comfort, and he comforts believers in their suffering.[9] This opening paragraph in 2 Corinthians illustrates well the close connection between the praise of God and God's power to sustain through suffering.

> Anybody can worship Santa Claus. But hanging in there with God in the midst of intense suffering, as Christ hung on the cross, magnifies the worth of God as the one who sustains us. God's goal in suffering, therefore, is to teach us that in life and death, as in all eternity, he himself is all we ultimately need. God never intends to destroy his people, nor will he allow anyone or anything else to do so. . . . In placing Paul in a situation in which he despaired even of life itself (2 Cor. 1:8), the only thing God destroyed was Paul's self-confidence. In return, Paul received God himself. In response, the apostle gave God praise.[10]

9. Hafemann, *2 Corinthians*, 58–78.
10. Ibid., 76.

Through Paul's suffering, he learned more about God, and he grew to trust him more and more. And the God of all comfort sustained and encouraged him in and through his suffering. Thus believers are able to comfort one another when they are in pain and are afflicted with the very same comfort they themselves have received from God. God's people, as they receive comfort from God in times of trouble, are able then to be a comfort and encouragement to others in their times of suffering.

One of the most precious experiences that I had during this illness was the encouragement that I received from God's people. I was blessed with comfort and encouragement from those whom God had allowed me to serve as a minister in the past. Many examples from this time in my life could be mentioned and many deserve to be mentioned, but I will describe two. Both of these encouragements and the comfort they offered me during my illness came from people whom I met while I served in my first full-time ministry in a church in Abington, Massachusetts. Through this encouragement from people whom I had served in ministry, I learned an important lesson about how God was able to meet my need in the midst of suffering and how he offered comfort and encouragement to me through his people. Some in whom I had invested time and had cultivated relationships were used by God to meet my need when I needed it the most.

Amy was a part of the young adult group at the first church where I served. She was a faithful member of that group who grew so much in Christ. It was a delight and an encouragement then to watch her growth in Christ. My wife and I had her in our home on a number of occasions for meals and conversation. She served in the ministries of that church. My wife and I count her as a friend whom we had the privilege to serve in the ministry of Christ's church. During some of the very dark days of my illness, she sent me a very simple card of encouragement, with a brief note written in it. She also had written a Scripture text in this card to encourage me: "Blessed is the man who perseveres under trial, because when he has stood the test, he will receive the crown of life that God has promised to those who love him" (Jas 1:12).

As a part of one of my classes at Oak Hills, I had taught the book of James that previous spring semester before my illness. In this class, I had stressed to my students the importance of the many teachings in Scripture on suffering and how to respond to it. Scripture does not teach us to ignore it, to pretend that it does not exist, or act as if it is not painful. And we do not endure suffering in a godly way as we "pull ourselves up by our own bootstraps," but we endure it as we trust in God and in his promises. I remember the day I received this card as a particularly rough day in terms of the effects of the chemotherapy, but I smiled when I read this card, and my heart was warmed with Scripture's encouragement. And I relished the delicious irony of this encouragement from Scripture to me in my suffering, an encouragement that I very recently had been emphasizing to my college students in much kinder and gentler times.

Todd was another young person who was part of this young adult ministry. Todd and I met often over the years to discuss life and Scripture, to read and discuss Christian books, and simply to enjoy good Christian friendship. Todd's eagerness to learn from Scripture and about theology were a great joy and delight for me, and I loved the opportunity to chat with him about life and to discuss biblical theology. His talents include singing and song writing. When I first met him, he eagerly offered his gifts in music as a contribution to our young adult ministry, and even our youth ministry. His musical gifts were clearly evident, and I asked him if he wrote any original music. He said that he didn't, at least any that he wished to share with me or with the church. So when he came to me a few months later and told me he had been working on a song, I agreed to listen to it with fairly low expectations. Todd himself had told me that he didn't write music. I remember well the Sunday morning when we sat in the senior pastor's office (which our young adult class used as a Sunday school room that year), and he played a song that reflected on the end of Isaiah 40. The song was unfinished, but he played what he had for me because he wanted to hear my response. My response was that he must finish this song within the next few weeks because we were leading a senior high youth group retreat then, and he must have this song ready to play for it. The basic message of this song and its message of hope in God from Isaiah 40 were the focus for this youth group retreat!

Todd has, over the years, produced three albums of original songs. I have always valued these musical gifts that God has given to him, and I have greatly benefited from their fruit. I very much appreciate the theologically grounded lyrics he writes. I often have been led in worship of God through his music. But especially during my illness, God used Todd's music to minister to me in powerful ways. God used Todd, someone I had encouraged in the faith in the past, to be a great encouragement to me in my suffering. Two songs in particular stand out.

The first song is entitled "Storm." I value this song so much because it creatively touches upon several important biblical themes, especially as it alludes to the stilling of the storm in the Gospels. It is an example of what I call biblical-theological lyrics. I include the complete lyrics, with permission, because of their significance for me:

A storm of such violence stole the silence from my day
It hit so hard, it knocked the wind right out of me
I've been rocked by its power from the hour I first drifted away
Without oars or anchor on the open sea

Now, taking on too much water, this ship is going down
Swallowed up in darkness by the sea and sky
While you lie sleeping, Jesus, I'm about to drown
Master, does it matter that I die?
Don't let me die

Jesus, King, Lord of the wind and rain
You can change these angry waves to glass again
'Cause at your will the demons flee
Just say the words, "Be still," and calm this sea
Oh, won't you stop this storm in me?
In me

My God, I have never felt so helpless before
I didn't know how hopeless I could be
It's like I'm too far gone to fight the good fight anymore
And the weight of these waves is crushing me

Jesus, King, Lord of the wind and rain
You can change these angry waves to glass again
'Cause at your will the demons flee
Just say the words, "Be still," and calm this sea
Oh, won't you stop this storm in me?
Will you save me? Will you save me?

Jesus, King, Lord of the wind and rain
You can change these angry waves

Jesus, King, Lord of the wind and rain
You can change these angry waves[11]

11. MacDonald, "Storm." Todd's music is available at http://www.toddmacdonald music.com.

Two things about this song ministered to me. First, its solidly biblical content written in a poetically creative way creates a vivid picture of this story from the Gospels. The lyrics allow one to imagine oneself actually in this boat as it is being overwhelmed by the waves. This song captures the heart of this narrative from the Gospels, and it presents it in a musically captivating way. Second, the lyrics focus on a prayer to God that is powerful. Like the lament psalms in Scripture, confidence is expressed in the one to whom the prayer is expressed. Yet the complaint directed to God is real and honest: "Master, does it matter that I die? Don't let me die!" In fact, in several places, the song is very direct in its petition to God: save me! It often became my prayer during my illness, and for a while I listened to it daily, sometimes several times a day.

The second song that God used to encourage and comfort me is entitled "The River Flows." I appreciate this song because of some of the conversations Todd and I have had over the years, conversations about the ebb and flow of faith in our lives. Again, this song creates a very clear and compelling image around which to encourage faith and trust in God during any and every circumstance of life. It describes Todd's love for the outdoors in such a way as to teach a spiritual lesson.

> So good just to get away
> For seven days on a river lost in Maine
> 'Cause like the water it's clear, Lord, that you are here
> And I am so glad I came
>
> So good just to let the river carry me
> But there's a lesson to be learned upon its waves
> Because the river rolls on, though not always so strong
> And that's just how my faith behaves
>
> Sometimes the river it flows high
> And sometimes the river it flows low
> Sometimes the river it flows white
> And sometimes the river it flows slow
>
> Ah . . . but the river flows
>
> River, run, and don't rest until you reach the sea
> Carry on for another night and day
> And know whenever I sing your song it'll bring
> New strength when I start to stray

Sometimes the river it flows high
And sometimes the river it flows low
Sometimes the river it flows white
And sometimes the river it flows slow

Ah . . . but the river flows on high and low
I've doubted it, but now I know
It's never dry; it never dies
I've finally come to realize
My faith comes from the faithful One
The sovereign Lord, the risen Son
And he has promised loud and clear
The saints will persevere

Sometimes the river it flows high
And sometimes the river it flows low
Sometimes the river it flows white
And sometimes the river it flows slow

Ah . . . but the river flows[12]

God used this song in my life to encourage trust in him when the river of faith seemed to run low or even to run dry. Sometimes my faith felt exactly like this. But on and on in perseverance it ran, even when it did not feel so. The encouragement toward perseverance in faith that I had been able to offer Todd from time to time in the past was returned to me then in powerful and effective ways as an encouragement to perseverance in faith and a comfort in a time of affliction. Todd comforted me with the comfort that he had received from God.

God used this young sister and brother in Christ to be a great encouragement to me when I was battling cancer. Amy and Todd both are people in whom God has worked and has comforted in their time of trial, and they both extended the compassion of Christ to me during my journey through a very dark valley. Two young people in whom God allowed me to invest part of my ministry life had been used by God to comfort me in my affliction. Those in whom I had invested my life in ministry were now investing in my encouragement in Christ. The God who comforts us in all our afflictions expects us to be a comfort to others who suffer. And he was the God of all comfort for me through Amy and Todd.

---

12. MacDonald, "The River Flows."

God has allowed me to extend comfort and encouragement to others who are facing affliction. I was very much aware that students especially were watching me during this struggle with cancer, and I trust that what they saw in me was a reflection of God's power as sufficient for me in my need and his power in the process of being perfected in my weakness (2 Cor 12:9). I have had conversations with many others who have had cancer, and those who have shared this experience are a mutual encouragement. I have found that, for me and for others who have endured cancer, there is a strange bond of shared experience, and sometimes it is just good to talk with someone who knows what this suffering is like. Such conversations have been an encouragement to me, and I know I have been able to encourage others who have or are facing a similar journey through a dark valley. Students and members of the church where I currently serve regularly approach me with their concern, and even fear, about a family member or a friend who has cancer. At the moment there are at least two students at the college who themselves are suffering through the treatment of cancer. I am sometimes still shocked at how many people are impacted by this horrible disease. But I am grateful to be able to comfort those who need it now because God has comforted me, even through those whom I served in ministry in the past.

I recently came across handwritten notes from my youngest two children that even now continue to be a great encouragement to me. These notes are an encouragement to me personally, but they are also an encouragement to me because of how God used my illness to encourage them to grow in Christ. I include them here exactly as they were written. The first is a Christmas wish list (I was in chemotherapy from August through January) from our youngest son, who was ten years old at the time (his nickname then was "frogboy" due, in part, to a pet frog that his older brother had given to him). It asked for one thing:

> Dear Mom and Dad,
> For X-mas all I want is for Dad to get better. Besides that, well, there isn't anything else. I'm praying for my wish to come true.
> Your loving son,
> Jeffrey, J.P. or Frogboy.
> P.S. Sorry for the messy writing, thank you for EVERYTHING.

The second is a note to me from our youngest daughter, who was nine years old. She wrote this note after we received the news that my cancer was in remission.

Dad,

I am so happy for you! In the beginning I was really scared. Sometimes I even cried. I know it's been hard. But with the churches help it's been easy for me. With my friends help I'm getting through it. Hope you get your strength back!

Sophia

God used this suffering for me and my family to accomplish something of spiritual significance in my children. Both learned at a fairly young age to trust and hope in God. And the recent remembrance of these notes has even now been another way that God has used this horrible experience to comfort and to encourage me. I am not happy for the experience of cancer, but I am very, very grateful for how God used this in the lives of Jeffrey and Sophia. This is a great comfort and encouragement to me.

December 13, 2005

It's just after noon, and I'm sitting in the outpatient room. Jeff is now in the O.R., under sedation, about to receive a port implant. This is something he didn't want. He really has cancer! Last week he had at least twenty-five needle pokes from the transfusion and other treatments. His poor veins are shot. There's scar tissue, and the chemo drugs are hard on his veins. I hate cancer!

We still don't have definite answers from the tests, and he still has one more test to undergo in Fargo. That's the P.E.T. scan.

Jeff is very weak. His legs are thin, and gravity is stronger than Jeff is right now. Yesterday we got a cane for him. It's a special one— hand made from diamond willow wood by my co-workers' uncle. He actually gave it to us; I was going to pay, but he said "no." It's beautiful!

I can't wait until this is over for Jeff. 'Till the doctor says, "it's gone, we got it." He has stage four cancer, but I have faith that God can heal Jeff. God can use these drugs to heal Jeff. I know deep down that it will be long and hard on Jeff and the whole family. I love Jeff, and I hate seeing him suffer. In my mind I can only think of him being healed. That's all. There will be life after cancer!

8

God's Timing

But Joseph said to them, "Do not fear, for am I in the place of God? As for you, you meant evil against me, but God meant it for good, to bring it about that many people should be kept alive, as they are today."

—GENESIS 50:19–20

December 13, 2005

Today is almost over. Jeff is home and doing fine. He's tired and worn out. But that's OK.

It was strange to see him being wheeled off today. I.V. in, questions answered, surgical garb in place—and then off he went. I stood in the room and watched the top of his head as he was rolled away to surgery. I just stood there in the middle of the big wide doorway feeling very lonely. When I realized the nurses were staring at me, I came to my senses, sat down and began writing all this. I'm glad this day is almost over.

Monday is the P.E.T. scan in Fargo. Then it's back to our "normal" schedule. No tests, just chemo every other Friday.

Joseph could not have anticipated how God would use his suffering for good. He had little chance to anticipate how God used the events of his life to put him exactly where God wanted him to help people during a famine. But the narrative of Joseph's life is clear on this point (Gen 37–50). The ups and downs of Joseph's life—his joys and his pain—all worked to put him exactly where God wanted him. God used what others had intended as evil and harm to have Joseph exactly in the right place at the right time. Even suffering could not stop or delay God's timing for his plan in relation to Joseph.[1]

---

1. Hafemann, *The God of Promise and the Life of Faith*, 77; and Carson, *How Long,*

The story is well known. Joseph is the favored son among twelve sons who is sold into slavery by his brothers. He is taken to Egypt, where he rises to prominence in Potiphar's house, as the overseer of his household. Joseph is falsely accused of an immoral relationship with Potiphar's wife, and he is sent to prison. While he is there, his skill as an interpreter of dreams lands him placement as a chief advisor and royal official in Pharaoh's court. There he is in a position to advise Pharaoh on the best course of action during a seven-year period of plenty to be followed by a seven-year period of famine. Thus, Joseph is in the right place at the right time to provide assistance to those who will suffer during a famine, including his own family! Even Joseph's suffering has a place in God's plan, or at the very least is not able to short-circuit that plan.

The narrative reaches a climax as Joseph confronts the brothers who have sold him into slavery (Gen 45:1–15). When they realize that the powerful man before whom they stand is the brother whom they had betrayed, they are rightly afraid. Joseph's response indicates his conviction that God has placed him here, despite or even because of their treachery. He responds to his brothers' fear with this encouragement:

> So Joseph said to his brothers, "Come near to me, please." And they came near. And he said, "I am your brother, Joseph, whom you sold into Egypt. And now do not be distressed or angry with yourselves because you sold me here, for God sent me before you to preserve life." (Gen. 45:4–5)

Joseph has a trust in the God who led him to this place to help people during a famine. To emphasize this belief in God and his plan, Joseph repeats this affirmation of trust in God and his plan: "And God sent me before you to preserve for you a remnant on earth, and to keep alive for you many survivors" (Gen 45:7).

> In the words of explanation and comfort to his brothers, Joseph returns once again to the central theme of the narrative: though the brothers intended "evil," God was ultimately behind it all and had worked it out for the "good". . . . Joseph's words pull back the narrative veil and allow the reader to see what has been going on behind the scenes. It was not the brothers who sent Joseph to Egypt—it was God. And God had a purpose for it all. We have seen numerous clues throughout the narrative that this has been the case, but now the central character . . . reveals the divine plans

---

O Lord? 205–6.

and purpose behind it all. Joseph, who can discern the divine plan in the dreams of Pharaoh, also knew the divine plan in the affairs of his brothers.[2]

Joseph, who is the interpreter of divine messages in dreams, has unique insight into God's plan and purpose for his life, including his suffering. This is the theological heart of the Joseph narrative.[3] For Joseph's family, of course, it was very important to preserve a remnant because God had made promises to them, beginning with Abraham in Genesis 12. God is committed to keeping his promises to Abraham. Joseph's conclusion is that God sent him to Egypt, not them: "So it was not you who sent me here, but God. He has made me a father to Pharaoh, and lord of all his house and ruler over all the land of Egypt" (Gen 45:8). Joseph has a trust that no matter what happened, God's timing for God's plan is sure and certain.

All is well and good for years as Joseph is reunited with his father, Jacob, and his brothers. They live together and prosper in Egypt. However, when Jacob died, his brothers' fears return because they reason, naturally, that Joseph may have been kind to them while their father was alive. Now that he has died, perhaps Joseph will exact revenge on them (Gen 50:15–21). They first send a message to Joseph in which they ask for forgiveness (Gen 50:16–17). Then they themselves approach their brother and plead with him (Gen 50:18). Joseph weeps when he realizes their fear of him, and he responds with an affirmation of his previously stated trust in God's sovereign plan and purpose for him: "But Joseph said to them, 'Do not fear, for am I in the place of God? As for you, you meant evil against me, but God meant it for good, to bring it about that many people should be kept alive, as they are today'" (Gen 50:19–20). What the brothers intended as evil and as harm for their brother, God intended for good to help many people during a famine. Joseph's reaffirmation of God's plan and purpose at work in and through his affliction, including the evil intent of his brothers, is the main point of this narrative.

> The statement about the brothers' evil plans and God's good plans now opens up the inmost mystery of the Joseph story. It is in every respect, along with the similar passage in ch. 45.5–7, the climax to the whole. Even where no man could imagine it, God had all the strings in his hand. But the guidance of God is only

2. Sailhamer, *The Pentateuch as Narrative*, 223.

3. von Rad, *Genesis*, 398–99; and Waltke, *Genesis*, 563.

asserted; nothing more explicit is said about the way in which God incorporated man's evil into his saving activity. The two statements "you meant . . ." and "God meant . . ." are ultimately very unyielding side by side.[4]

Joseph is indeed in God's place for him despite their evil intent. The assertions of the Joseph narrative that his brothers meant evil but God meant good must be held in tension in order to respect the narrative of this story. Both are asserted without much, if any, attempt to reconcile them. Joseph's brothers are responsible for their actions, but God is able to accomplish his own good plan and purpose despite their evil actions. God's timing, even when everything in Joseph's life seemed to becoming unhinged, is perfect.[5]

I was diagnosed with a very advanced form of Hodgkin's Lymphoma after one year of teaching at Oak Hills Christian College. By the time the doctor diagnosed this disease, it had already spread to my bone marrow. Three things about my particular experience with this disease were atypical. First, a lymphoma usually moves from lymph node to lymph node throughout a person, moving from station to station like a train on its tracks, until it finally reaches the internal organs and/or the bone marrow. My cancer was only in the lymph nodes in my left armpit and then had taken the "express route" directly to my bone marrow. My oncologist informed me that this pattern for my Hodgkin's Lymphoma was a highly unusual progression for this disease and that he did not have an explanation for it. Second, this Hodgkin's Lymphoma typically strikes a much younger or a much older person. Young people more typically are diagnosed, and it is fairly rare for someone older than the late twenties to have this disease. Or senior citizens can also more typically be diagnosed. It is unusual for a middle-aged man to get this. And third, the particular kind of Hodgkin's Lymphoma that I had is relatively rare. I remember my doctor telling me that about seventy thousand cases of Lymphoma are diagnosed in the United States each year and about seven thousand cases of Hodgkin's Lymphoma are diagnosed. My particular kind of Hodgkin's Lymphoma (lymphocyte predominant) accounts for only five percent of the diagnoses of this disease in the United States each year—only a few hundred cases. This cancer was rare and unusual for several reasons, any one of which would have made it atypical. In my

---

4. von Rad, *Genesis*, 432.

5. Sailhamer, *The Pentateuch as Narrative*, 239; and Waltke, *Genesis*, 623–24.

case, there were three unique and rare sets of circumstances. It was like the disease equivalent of hitting the lottery!

The form and progression of this cancer certainly were not typical, and the timing of its diagnosis seemed to make no sense to me at all. *Why now, God?* was a frequent thought on my mind then. God had called me to move sixteen hundred miles away from where we had lived for about fifteen years, during seminary and in service of two churches in Massachusetts. While we lived there, we were very close to a great number of very fine medical facilities, including some of the best cancer treatment facilities in the country. We had a church family, both local and extended, that had been cultivated over many years, and we had friends in the local community. Many fine resources were available there to help us during my treatment for this disease. Yet barely a year later we faced this deadly disease apparently alone, having been uprooted to a new community located in a small, rural town in a fairly remote part of northern Minnesota. We were seemingly so far from access to the medical help we needed. Bemidji, Minnesota, has a regional hospital and a medical clinic, but initially it appeared to be fairly remote and a considerable distance from the medical help I needed. The Roger Maris Cancer Center in Fargo, North Dakota, is several hours away. Medical facilities in the Twin Cities are a four-hour drive from Bemidji. The Mayo Clinic in Rochester, Minnesota, is more than six hours away. We appeared to be isolated from the medical help I needed. And despite the kindness of colleagues, neighbors, and friends in Bemidji, it seemed that we were nearly two thousand miles from most of the people we knew best. We were just beginning to settle into this community and to establish relationships at work, in our community, and at church. It felt very much like we were alone in this valley. I regularly fought the thought that God had brought me here to die.

Yet we were exactly where God wanted us to be. It became painfully clear very early in my chemotherapy that this treatment was going to take an extreme toll on my body. Physically, it left me exhausted, to say the least. Walking any distance grew increasingly difficult. On the few occasions when I had to travel any great distance in a car, I actually thought I would die during the trip. This is no exaggeration, as my wife can attest. If we had remained in Massachusetts, we would have been near the fine cancer treatment facilities in Boston; but these would have been about a seventy-mile trip each way on the Massachusetts Turnpike, which could take a couple of hours round trip, or more, each direction, if the traffic was congested. In Bemidji, I soon learned, I was about two miles from the oncology clinic where I received almost all of my treatments and tests. It was about a five-minute trip. It could only have been more convenient if the doctor and nurses had come to my home for my treatment! God knew where we needed to be.

In chapter 6, I mentioned the care and concern expressed to me by the Oak Hills Christian College community. Despite the fact that we were very new, we were treated in this town as though we had been friends for a very long time. We were embraced with a very generous spirit in the college community and in our church. From people at my wife's workplace and in our community here in Bemidji, we experienced the love and compassion of many, many generous people. Meals were prepared and delivered and assistance was given with yard work. There were many, many more acts of kindness, as well. We really felt as though we had been a part of this community for many years instead of the twelve months that we had lived here.

Early in my chemotherapy, my oncologist recommended a second opinion on my diagnosis and treatment plan. He did not recommend this second opinion because he had any great doubts about his diagnosis, although he did admit that he is fallible and welcomed another doctor to double check his diagnosis. He recommended this second opinion from the leading specialist in the country on my particular kind of cancer so that, based on his evaluation and recommendation, I might receive a newer drug in my chemotherapy that had already received F.D.A. approval for treatment of more common Lymphomas. This drug, Rituximub (also known as Rituxan), was a newer kind of cancer drug that, as I understand my doctor's explanation, worked with my immune system to trick cancer cells. It worked alongside my body's own defenses to identify individual cancer cells. It then sent a signal to each individual cancer cell that turned off the mechanism that caused it to feed on my body so that the cancer actually starved itself. Each individual cancer cell was targeted and tricked into no longer feeding on the healthy cells in my body until each cancer cell eventually died. Unlike conventional chemotherapy that attacks everything that grows rapidly in the body, healthy or not, Rituximub targeted individual cancer cells and left healthy cells alone. I have described it as the "smart bomb" of cancer treatment, in sharp contrast with conventional chemotherapy that is more like Napalm!

But Rituximub was very expensive, costing more than sixty-eight hundred dollars for each treatment. My particular kind of cancer, my doctor explained, was so rare it was not likely to be the subject of a clinical trial and so insurance companies might not agree to pay for the cost without an expert's recommendation. But he thought there was every reason to think that I might benefit from this newer treatment, if the traditional chemotherapy did not completely remove this cancer from my body. He wanted me to seek a second opinion on my diagnosis and treatment, with the hope that a leading expert on Hodgkin's Lymphoma might confirm the diagnosis and a treatment plan that would include Rituximub. Based on this specialist's recommendation, my insurance might be more likely to pay for this new treatment for Lymphoma. As my oncologist was explaining this proposed plan for a second opinion to us in his office, my wife and I fully expected to hear that this specialist was back on the East Coast, perhaps even in the Boston area. I was already beginning to think about travel plans and their cost as my doctor discussed this with us. Instead, much to our surprise he informed us that this specialist worked at the University of Minnesota in Minneapolis. The expert on my particular cancer, which was very, very rare, worked in the closest major city to Bemidji, and God had moved us here one year ago.

God had us right where he wanted us, where I could receive good treatment in the most convenient manner and where I could have more easy access to an expert's second opinion on my diagnosis and treatment. Another way God worked his timing for my benefit was in a more personal and private way. My youngest brother, Mike, reached a milestone birthday in the summer of 2005. My parents, siblings, and nephews had traveled from Texas to Massachusetts during the previous summer to attend our oldest daughter's high school graduation ceremony and celebration. During her graduation party, Mike was chatting with our dad about his desire to see a game at Wrigley Field for his birthday that next summer. Dad told him that perhaps they could take a road trip to see a game and, if they were to go to the trouble of driving that far, maybe they should see a few games on the way up and back. My brother, Greg, overheard this conversation and asked to join the fun. At this point, I was approached to join the trip, and the Wisdom guys' summer baseball trip was born!

Plans were made to see a game in St. Louis, Chicago, Milwaukee, and Kansas City, along with a stop for a minor league game in Des Moines and a visit to the location for the film *Field of Dreams* in Dyersville, Iowa. The dates in the 2005 baseball season for the trip were selected to ensure games at the stadiums on this midwestern circuit. Dad purchased tickets online to secure the best seats for us. Hotel reservations were made in advance. Plans for time off from work were secured. A plane ticket was purchased for me to travel to St. Louis to meet them there on Saturday, the day before the first game of this trip. This baseball trip for a dad and his three sons was set in February for August 6 through August 12 of that year.

When I was diagnosed with this cancer in July of that summer, the prospects for this trip seemed to be over for me. It did not seem to me that it would be possible for me to join the fun. But I really wanted to travel on this trip with my dad and brothers. I called my dad to let him know that I might not be able to make the trip. On several occasions I remarked to friends who knew of the plans for this trip that I would rather die than miss it. And I was only joking, in part. Once Chris overheard me say this (actually I said it once so she could overhear it!), and she just slapped me in the back. I really, really wanted to go on this trip, but frankly did not see how this was possible, given the tests that were ahead of me. There would be tests to diagnose this cancer and tests to determine how advanced it was. And as I projected a tentative timeline from late July through early August, this seemed inevitably to collide with this week and this trip.

My oncologist also was not enthusiastic about this trip when I mentioned it to him. With respect to my disease and its treatment, he was all business. He wanted to move the tests and the treatment to follow along as quickly as possible. These tests would be over the last few weeks of July and the first week or two of August—in a direct collision course with this trip. I appreciated his concern and diligence then and appreciate it even more so now. But still, I wanted to make this trip work. As the final tests were scheduled, the last one was a bone marrow biopsy on the Friday that was the day before I was to fly out of Bemidji. When the doctor told me that the results would not be available for three to five business days, I saw my opportunity. The earliest the test results would be back was on Wednesday of the week of this trip, and perhaps they would not be back until Friday, the day I was to return to Bemidji.

Surely, I reasoned with my doctor, a day or two would not matter that much in the end. Otherwise, I would just be sitting around and waiting to hear the results. Wouldn't it be better for me, at least a better distraction for me, to enjoy this trip?

He agreed. So the day after I had a bi-lateral bone marrow biopsy in which marrow was extracted from both of my hip bones, I was on a flight out of Bemidji and was heading for St. Louis. This trip was exactly what I needed at that exact time. I had the opportunity to share the news of this disease with my two brothers in person, and I had a great time at the ballparks, during our travels, and in our visits to these midwestern cities. I returned to Bemidji on the next Friday and went directly from the airport to the doctor's office to hear the stage of this cancer and the prescribed treatment plan. I began chemotherapy the next Wednesday. If this trip—whose inception had been more than a year earlier and which had been finalized months in advance to take place during this first week of August—had been a week earlier or a week later, I could not have gone. But it came at just the right time in the sequence of events from diagnosis to the beginning of treatment. The timing for this trip could not have been more perfect. It is as though it was part of the plan for my diagnosis and treatment.

It was a great trip. I saw David Eckstein hit a walk-off grand slam in the final season of Busch Stadium. I saw Ken Griffey Jr. hit a home run into the left centerfield bleachers in Wrigley Field. I took batting practice and played catch on the Field of Dreams with my dad and brothers. I got to hang out with them and to enjoy their company for a week. This is something that I had not been able to do very often, and I had a great week with them. God gave me the chance to go on this trip that was, at the very least, a pleasant distraction from simply waiting and waiting for test results. I am glad I went.

I do not have all the answers about why God allowed me to get sick. I am not making a claim that I do have such answers. If I could have changed things, I would never have allowed cancer to touch my life. There are parts of this whole experience that I don't really understand, and much of it that I still do not like at all. But at least some of God's timing in all of this seems clear to me. A move to northern Minnesota seemed at first to have relocated me to a remote place simply to die, but instead, it in fact moved me very close to convenient medical facilities, fine doctors and nurses, and a specialist on the particularly rare cancer that I had. When I was ill, I was in just the right place at just the right time for me and my family. And God even allowed the pleasant diversion of a baseball trip with my dad and my brothers to fit into this timing. I still have questions, but God has allowed me to see enough of his plan to continue to inspire my trust in him.

December 20, 2005

We made it to Fargo and back just fine. It was a long day at the Roger Maris Cancer Center. They were really busy! I drove the whole way—now I know Jeff feels crappy because he loves to drive!

I guess today he will stay at the college all day to give two final exams. One of which I should be taking, but instead I'm going to Jeffrey's and Sophia's Christmas program. Tim's was last night. Meg comes home tomorrow and Bri maybe the next day, Thursday. But Friday for sure.

I woke up praying this morning. Everything gushed. A thankful heart for all those who have given us money, food, and childcare, prepared meals and support! Thankful that Bri and Meg are coming home. For safety when they travel, and of course for Jeff. I forgot how to pray for a while and have been depending on the prayers of others. But this morning I was praying as I was waking up.

I have a long "to do" list and notes to write, plus I'd like to send out Christmas cards, but we'll see.

We may know the results of all the tests this Friday. If they aren't good, I don't want to know. I want to keep my focus on Christ this Christmas—not poor us, poor Jeff, poor kids or poor me. I'm, frankly, afraid to know! I'm just too afraid to know!

PART THREE

Biblical-Theological Reflections on the Struggle Experienced during a Season of Suffering

9

Forgotten by God?

How long, O LORD? Will you forget me forever?
How long will you hide your face from me?
How long must I take counsel in my soul
and have sorrow in my heart all the day?
How long shall my enemy be exalted over me?

Consider and answer me, O LORD my God;
light up my eyes, lest I sleep the sleep of death.

—PSALM 13:1–3

September 27, 2005
   . . . *Pretty bad. Today I took Jeff to E.R. with temperature of 103.1°. He has flu symptoms. He received one bag of saline or sodium chloride. They did a bunch of blood work, chest x-ray, urine test—everything came back good. But he's fighting some small infection somewhere in his body. He feels crummy!*

September 30, 2005
   . . . *Somewhat better. But still a bad week!*

October 3, 2005
   Better, but he is really tired. Hasn't been out of bed much the whole week. His chest C.T. results came back and they weren't good. They look like cotton candy. The Bleomycin was causing minor lung damage and a fever of 103.8° on Tuesday evening.

October 10, 2005
   . . . *We took a fifteen-minute walk tonight, and Jeff was so out of breath when we got back. He's not feeling well. Tired and no energy.*

October 11, 2005

The drugs are wiping him out! Will it be the cancer or the chemo that brings him down? With each treatment he is more and more tired. More and more unable to stay out of bed. How will he be able to teach even one class next semester at this rate? I wonder if I'll be able to work or if I'll have to stay home and care for him full time. I will do it in a minute, but I don't want him so sick.

The Twenty-third Psalm affirms a confidence that God is with his people even through the valley of the shadow of death. He is a good shepherd who is always present with his people and provides for them. This is the affirmation of Scripture, and it is often a great comfort to God's people. But sometimes they do not feel that divine presence with them in the midst of their suffering. I certainly did not. The experience of suffering sometimes causes people to wonder if God has forgotten them. Had God forgotten me?

This sense of God's apparent absence in a time of trouble was one of the most surprising experiences for me during this time of suffering. Prior to my diagnosis with a stage IV cancer, the most serious medical issue that I had personally ever faced was either the removal of a couple of ingrown toenails when I was a teenager or the simple removal of a couple of wisdom teeth when I was an adult. I had never injured a knee or an ankle when I played sports in my youth. I had never had a surgery, nor had I ever spent a night in the hospital. I really rarely needed to see the doctor because, until this illness, I had lived a life that was basically healthy and free of injury. But now I found myself confronted with a disease that could claim my life. I went from an ingrown toenail or a wisdom tooth extraction to a stage IV cancer; it was like I went from first gear into overdrive without shifting through second, third, and fourth gears! It was a jolt, to say the least.

But it is not merely that this came as a surprise to me, but rather this surprise carried along with it the seeds of doubt. Os Guinness puts his finger directly on the problem when he writes, "'Where is God?' is urgent for faith because the question that for the skeptic is an attack on someone else's faith is anguish for the believer because it is an assault on his own."[1] C. S. Lewis captures the experience of the sense of abandonment as only he can:

1. Guinness, *Unspeakable*, 63.

> Meanwhile, where is God? This is one of the most disquieting symptoms. When you are happy, so happy that you have no sense of needing Him, so happy that you are tempted to feel His claims upon you as an interruption, if you remember yourself and turn to Him with gratitude and praise, you will be—or so it feels—welcomed with open arms. But go to Him when your need is desperate, when all other help is vain, and what do you find? A door slammed in your face, and a sound of bolting and double bolting on the inside. After that, silence. You may as well turn away. The longer you wait, the more emphatic the silence will become. There are no lights in the windows. It might be an empty house. Was it ever inhabited? It seems so once. And that seeming was as strong as this. What can this mean? Why is He so present a commander in our time of prosperity and so very absent a help in time of trouble?[2]

Sometimes Christians, in my past experiences in the church, have seemed to me too quick to dismiss or disregard this because it may seem to some to border on a God-dishonoring attitude—to disrespect God and to fail to trust him. But I think that it is possible to hold on to our affirmation of God's presence with us as well as our honest lament and even fear that God has forgotten us and our situation in time of trouble. It is possible to have, at the same time, a trust in God and an honest expression of exactly what we are experiencing in our fragile humanity. The lament during suffering that is recorded in the Psalms and in the accounts of some who suffered instructs us that this is an honest and valid question.

Certainly an absolute denial of God's presence with us in suffering is not what I have in mind here; instead, I am thinking of the genuine experience of a failure to perceive his presence with me when I am in the valley of the shadow of death.[3] This seems to me to be the very clear implication of the question: "How long, O Lord? Will you forget me forever? How long will you hide your face from me?" (Ps 13:1). This question is posed four times in rapid succession, and it gives this psalm a sense of the intensity of the suffering that is assaulting the petitioner.[4] The psalmist is facing enemies who oppose him, seek to bring him into submission, and probably even seek to kill him (Ps 13:2–4).

2. Lewis, *A Grief Observed*, 5–6.

3. Terrien, *The Elusive Presence*.

4. Goldingay, *Psalms*, 1:205.

The questions express the sense that God has withdrawn from the psalmist's present experience and has hidden himself. God's failure to appear and act leads to a fear of abandonment—that Yahweh has forgotten the psalmist. Such divine forgetfulness threatens to undo him, because to be known and remembered by God is to be in the relationship of blessing (as Ps. 1:6 clearly suggests).[5]

Verse 2 highlights both the internal and external threats to the faithful.[6] The internal experience reflected in this psalm is that one is left to one's own thoughts and plans ("How long must I take counsel in my soul . . . ?") and that sorrow is a daily and constant companion ("and [how long] have sorrow in my heart all the day?"). The external experience is the apparent certainty, given the Lord's absence, that the enemies will ultimately prevail ("How long shall my enemy be exalted over me?"). Psalm 13 reflects an experience that God is silent and absent, and it honestly wonders how long he will remain so.[7]

How can a person hold together a trust in God along with an honest expression of the pain experienced and the sense that God has forgotten? One way is to follow the example of this psalm and present our dilemma directly to God himself! Psalm 13 does not talk *about* God who seems to have forgotten, but rather it speaks directly *to* God who seems to have forgotten and who seems absent. It is a very important point that this psalm does not speak about God, but addresses him directly. When we speak directly to a person, we do so because we expect, at least to some extent, to be heard and to have a response from the one who hears our voice and our heart. This response may not always be what we have in mind, but we speak to a person to get a response. Psalm 13 addresses God, it does not speak about him; and this is implicitly an affirmation of faith that God listens, at least.

There may be a variety of reasons that we do not speak honestly and openly with another person when we are suffering and in pain, especially if that person is somehow connected closely to our suffering or is even somehow connected to the cause of our pain. Perhaps someone we care about is either to some extent responsible for the pain we experience or knows at least something of the situation we face and could respond, but hasn't done so. If we care enough about that other person, we may,

5. Wilson, *Psalms*, 1:278.

6. Ibid., 278–79.

7. Goldingay, *Psalms*, 1:206.

in some situations, hold back some of our honesty so that we don't hurt him or her because our complete honesty may be a burden too difficult to carry. To be completely honest in some situations with some people may be too brutal to bear. After all, they are only human! They could be hurt by our words; and if we care enough about them, we may wish to shield them from this. If we care about them, we would not want to hurt them unnecessarily. Perhaps they could not bear the weight of our honest expression of pain. Sometimes we may want to protect people we care about from pain and suffering, and so we hold back from the honest expression of our heart.

Sometimes I wonder if we don't often treat God as though he were really like us in our fragile egos and in our emotional needs, and even our emotional instability. We would never say this, of course. But in our actions and attitudes we may often betray this perspective on God. Why do we hold back from the honest expression of our pain when we talk with another person? As I have suggested, perhaps it is that sometimes we are afraid that this person may not be able to handle this honesty. Perhaps we may hurt or offend this person in some way, especially if this person bears even a small part in the responsibility for our pain or is in some way reasonably expected to respond appropriately and helpfully to it, but has not. Certainly God knows everything about our situation, and yet sometimes he seems to hide himself. This is certainly the heart of the complaint in Psalm 13. This psalm does not doubt that God knows the situation; it expresses a question about whether or not God intends to act on behalf of the one who trusts in him.[8]

Sometimes we hold back from honesty because those we care about do not really know what we are facing, and we choose to carry a burden alone rather than lay it unnecessarily on those we love. But this never applies to God; he knows everything about what we are facing better than we do. Or we may hold back at times because we don't want to hurt or offend the other person. People may sometimes be too small to hear our honest lament, but God is not like us in our human weaknesses. Or sometimes when the pain is too great, perhaps we express this hurt simply to vent frustration and anger, not really so much to be heard. Sometimes people may not be able to hear this honest expression of frustration without harmful effects, but God is willing and able to hear our honest lament. None of these concerns that hold us back from hon-

8. Ibid.

est lament seem appropriate in our conversation with God. And Psalm 13 provides us both with a model and with an encouragement to include lament in our conversation with God.

This is, indeed, what Psalm 13 does. It moves from the honest expression of complaint to the direct expression of request: "Consider and answer me, O Lord my God; light up my eyes, lest I sleep the sleep of death, lest my enemy say, 'I have prevailed over him,' lest my foes rejoice because I am shaken" (Ps 13:3–4). This psalm offers an honest complaint to God ("how long?") and an honest prayer to God (if you don't act, I will die!).[9] This petition conveys a sense of urgency that God must give attention and no longer remain silent.[10] Thus Psalm 13 is completely honest with God; it expresses the specific frustration with the situation and the directly honest request to remedy this trouble.

Psalm 13 does more than talk to God honestly, though. It also expresses a deeply rooted trust in him despite what is experienced: "But I have trusted in your steadfast love; my heart shall rejoice in your salvation. I will sing to the Lord, because he has dealt bountifully with me" (Ps 13:5–6). Psalm 13 professes trust in the Lord's "steadfast love," which implies trust in the Lord's rock-solid commitment to his people.[11] The Lord is trustworthy despite what circumstance or emotion may tell us. In this psalm, both the voicing of pain and confession of trust stand together. They apparently are not contradictory, but they complement one another.

> Psalm 13 shows that trust does issue in insistent questioning of God that asks why God is ignoring us in our need, and in urgent pressing of God to give us attention and brighten our eyes with the promise of action. As before, this action does not belong just in the great past and the eschatological future. It belongs to now.[12]

The honest expression of pain and the expression of honest questions toward God accompany the directly brutal questions: "How long, O Lord?" "Will you forget me forever?" and "How long will you hide your face from me?" (Ps 13:1). The honest question directed to God in the midst of suffering can itself be an expression of trust in him.

9. Wilson, *Psalms*, 1:279.
10. Goldingay, *Psalms*, 1:207.
11. Wilson, *Psalms*, 1:279.
12. Goldingay, *Psalms*, 1:209.

One of the things that I learned is that I do not always know what God is doing in my life. And I do not understand why God sometimes leaves us in severe suffering for so long. In fact, I have grown increasingly suspicious of people who confidently claim to know God's plan and purpose for virtually every circumstance in life, especially in the midst of suffering. I have grown especially suspicious of those who claim to know this for others who are walking through some very deep and dark valleys. Such experts on the suffering that others endure remind me too much of Job's friends who clearly do not see the cause and reason for Job's suffering very well![13] I do not always know what God is doing in my own life, and why he sometimes seems so absent in the midst of trouble. But I may trust that God knows and he is working, even when all this remains very unclear to me. Everything we face is not good, but God is good and is not overwhelmed by the suffering inflicted on his people by a fallen world. The Apostle Paul affirms this confidence: "And we know that for those who love God all things work together for good, for those who are called according to his purpose" (Rom 8:28). In this context Paul has described the suffering and pain now in a fallen world, a passage we have previously considered in this book. Believers suffer (Rom 8:18), groan in their troubles along with a personified fallen world (Rom 8:23), and experience weakness (Rom 8:26). All things indeed are not good, but God is able to work them together for what is good for those who love him and are called according to his purpose. I trust that this is true even when everything that I am feeling and experiencing leaves me cold and feeling very much alone. Sometimes the pain and suffering seem to overwhelm, and God seems distant or absent.

Before I came to Oak Hills Christian College, I was the pastor of a small church in New England. Shortly before I left this ministry to move to Minnesota, Debbie was diagnosed with cancer. Her disease was very aggressive, and there was no prescribed, standard treatment for it. So she told me the doctors treated it like another, similar cancer. Debbie was a member of this church, and even before her diagnosis she was regularly involved in worship and actively engaged in the study of Scripture. She was a believer in Jesus Christ with a love for the Lord and a love for his Word. I had the privilege of watching her grow and mature in her faith.

---

13. Lawson, *Job*, 9, 11; Carson, *How Long, O Lord?* 161–68; and Hafemann, *The God of Promise and the Life of Faith*, 154–61.

Toward the end of my treatment for cancer, I called Debbie and we chatted about life. As you may imagine, we shared and compared stories about the ordeal of cancer and its treatment. I have called this the sharing of "war stories"! She had had it far worse than I did, with multiple rounds of chemotherapy over several years. But still I could understand and sympathize with her, much more than I had been able to before my illness. During this phone conversation I told her directly that I think that I would be a very different pastor for her now than I had been then. I think that I had done the best that I could possibly have done, but things would be different now. They would be very different, indeed.

During the course of our conversation, Debbie shared with me the increasing difficulty that the nurses were having in starting an I.V. line for chemotherapy. I understood this because I had the same trouble during my treatment. I had gone into chemo with a lifelong aversion to needles into veins, something that had its roots in a bad experience during childhood involving routine blood work, a young Air Force nurse, and repeated poking and wiggling to find (unsuccessfully!) a vein in either arm. As a result, I think my veins spent most of the rest of my life in hiding. Some things, though, you simply must get accustomed to. One nurse called me a "hard stick," because my veins were difficult to find. After four months of treatment, I needed a transfusion of two units of irradiated, compacted red blood cells. A larger than usual needle was needed for this, a needle that felt like the size of a garden hose. After this transfusion, my veins were so shot that the doctor ordered an I.V. port, which required a minor surgical procedure. This made the I.V. line process quick and simple. After my surgery, the operating room nurse recommended that I ask my doctor about a Lidocaine and Prilocaine cream for the skin that stretched over this port. It is a simple stick of a needle, but this cream helped to numb the area just enough. And she reasoned, "why go through any more pain than is needed?" I agreed with her!

When I spoke with Debbie, she lamented the increasing pain she felt over the years from repeated use of her port. She had a couple installed because eventually one would stop working well, and she would need another. And she would also develop bruising from the more constant use of her port. I had found the cream for my port a convenience. I had forgotten to use it once or twice, and it was a minor needle poke and nothing more. It sounded like Debbie could really use this cream. I asked her if she had heard of it, but she had not. I told her that I thought this was barbaric—to allow her to suffer a needless pain when an inexpensive cream could provide relief. She told me that she would look into it. I was glad that I was able to be of some practical help to her, at least.

That was the last time that I spoke with Debbie. She died on February 20, 2007—the same day that I learned that my cancer was still in remission during my one-year doctor's appointment. I had been especially nervous about this doctor's visit. When I began my regular appointments and tests, which came every three months, I was so tired and worn down by the cancer and its treatment that I sort of expected that this news of remission was a temporary reprieve. I was a bit pessimistic, I will admit. It took me six months even to begin to feel a little bit normal again. As the one-year appointment and tests approached, I told Chris that I really needed to get past this one with good news. I never allowed myself to assume that this was all over. I might need to go back into chemo, or I might need other treatments in the future. And I needed to be prepared for this possibility.

In the first year after chemotherapy I never allowed myself to assume that the recent good news that we had of remission meant that this was all over. Emotionally, I don't think that I could have borne the disappointment. I called this the "keeping my game face on" approach. One specific way this approach manifested itself in daily living is that I kept my hair trimmed short. I really did not want to go through the process of losing my hair again, so I kept it trimmed very short. Actually, I learned over time that I liked the fact that I did not need to worry about my hair in the morning and that I no longer needed to carry a comb. I realized that there are very, very few "perks" that go along with chemotherapy, but one for me is that I no longer needed to concern myself with my hair!

When we learned at the one-year mark that the tests continued to show no evidence of cancer in my body, it was a happy day. After this news, I typically joked with my students at the college that, despite all of the anecdotal evidence to the contrary, the doctor continued to insist that I was normal! Well, he insisted that my test results were normal; he was not vouching for my personality or my sanity! I was so relieved and happy for this news. And the every three-month schedule for doctor's visits and tests would change for this second year to be every six months, so I had at least six months before it was even possible to go back into chemotherapy.

That night the phone rang. It was a friend from the same church that I had served and in which Debbie had worshipped. She had died that very day. I still don't quite know exactly how to feel about this. Joy and happiness were tempered, but they were still there. There was sadness that Debbie had suffered this ordeal, along with relief that her suffering with this cancer in this life was over. There was hope for her, the Christian hope of the resurrection when Debbie will be raised to an immortal, incorruptible body. This is the hope that all believers share. Happiness, sadness, and hope all mingled together that day in me in a rare and precious mixture.

My conversation with Debbie was a great encouragement to me, and I trust she also was encouraged. I have found that my conversations with others who have gone through cancer are always a great encouragement, even if the actual conversation topics are not about things that are very pleasant. On that day in February, the question of Psalm 13 was answered for Debbie and for me in two very different ways. Debbie passed into the Lord's presence, and she no longer suffered with cancer. She is with the Lord and awaits the Christian hope of the resurrection. I learned that God had graciously given me another year without cancer here on this earth. I continue to walk by faith in the Lord who is my shepherd. I walk with him by faith, and I look forward, in hope, to the resurrection when I will receive an immortal, incorruptible body. I trust that the Lord is my shepherd even if I must again walk through the valley of the shadow of death. I trust that he is my shepherd who hears me when I ask

> How long, O Lord? Will you forget me forever?
>   How long will you hide your face from me?
> How long must I take counsel in my soul
>   and have sorrow in my heart all the day?
> How long shall my enemy be exalted over me?
>
> Consider and answer me, O Lord my God;
>   light up my eyes, lest I sleep the sleep of death. (Ps 13:1–3)

These questions do not call trust in God into question when they are the honest expression of the pain that the believer is experiencing. These questions should, indeed must, be the lament of God's people—the lament that is spoken directly to him. They are an important part of the walk of faith.

October 26, 2005

. . . Very tired! Very emotional! A side of Jeff that I've never seen. He's still breathing hard at times, and most times his mouth is sore. His temperature goes up and down, which frustrates him. He's had a sick stomach this time.

November 13, 2005

Thursday was chemo day. After the next one Jeff will have tests to see how effective the treatment has been. I can't wait, yet I don't want to be disappointed. Jeff feels the same way and is also afraid to hear the results. The side effects are so powerful now. With each treatment, they are worse. Sometimes depression sets in. He's very weak and is barely able to get up and down stairs. When he's really tired, he shakes, a lot. Even his mouth shakes when he tries to talk. It's like he's shivering. Some days he talks non-stop. Other days he's very quiet—I know he's going through this valley alone.

10

I Want to be on That Committee!

Oh, the depth of the riches and wisdom and knowledge of God!
How unsearchable are his judgments and how inscrutable his ways!
  "For who has known the mind of the Lord,
  or who has been his counselor?" ꙮ꙯ ᴧ 40
  "Or who has given a gift to him that he might be repaid?"
For from him and through him and to him are all things.
To him be glory forever. Amen.

—ROMANS 11:33–36

November 21, 2005
  Jeff has been so sick this last week. I think he got my sinus infection and cough, and for that I feel awful! He is on penicillin. Jeff has been running a temperature, as high as 101.2°. I'm so glad he had to go to see the oncologist for something else, because he saw him and gave him an antibiotic. Hopefully he will be well enough to receive the chemo on Friday. He has been coughing so hard and so much! His stomach muscles are sore. He has so much cold medicine in him that everything tastes nasty! Besides the chemo that makes everything taste nasty! I hope by Thursday he is better. That's Thanksgiving Day! Then chemo on Friday. Jeff is physically very weak. He stumbled getting up from the computer desk at home, and he said he went down on his face—but he didn't really fall. I fear the day when he falls down the stairs at work because his thighs aren't strong enough to hold him up. A broken bone would be the worst thing for him now! Or a cut—that would be bad too!

December 20, 2005
  It's 5:45 a.m., and Jeff's still sleeping so I don't know how he's feeling today. Do I really know how he's feeling? Not really, but I write what I see. I think the blood transfusion he had has helped, but he

is still very weak. He uses a cane to steady himself. Mainly to walk up and down stairs and to have some extra stability by his side. I know he doesn't really like being so weak that he needs to use a cane. I think he's in the part of the cycle where his emotions go weird on him. He's angry, short tempered, and tearful. He is still uncomfortable about having a port put in and now that it's in, it hurts. His shoulder is sore, but it's beginning to heal. He will have at least one more surgery . . . to remove the port.

I know he's sick of the whole ordeal and many times has wanted to give up, but he keeps on going.

A pastor once gave me some advice for pastoral ministry. This pastor had many, many years of experience in ministry and had been serving his current church for two decades. So I eagerly listened to this voice of experience when he offered some advice. He suggested that I always serve on the nominating committee of the church that I served. The nominating committee sought out people to serve in various other capacities in this church, and they recommended these people for approval at our annual business meeting. Rarely did a nomination come from the floor at this annual meeting (actually this never happened, to the best of my memory). And the vote of the church members typically approved all those who had been nominated. So this committee had a tremendous influence on who served and where they served in this church.

This pastor with many years' experience in ministry recommended that this is my practice every year—which I serve on the nominating committee. It seemed an odd bit of counsel to me at the time. But, he continued, this way the pastor can help to direct people to the right places to serve that best match their gifts and experience. The pastor does not pick people to serve on various committees, but he is allowed to participate in the process before this becomes too public. It also allows the pastor to discourage, and even prevent, some people from serving on a particular committee and choosing to serve on a particular committee, Christian Education for example, because they are unhappy about some recent decisions or about a current course of direction for a ministry of the church. This pastor had some experience with church members who tried to get their own way in the decisions and direction of the church through strategic membership on just the right committees. Can you imagine that in the church?

I took this pastor's advice, but reluctantly. I did not follow his counsel right away after our conversation, but after a year or two. I was a somewhat reluctant to try this because it seemed to me to be a bit pessimistic about people in the church and their motives for service within the church, but I tried it nevertheless. I am not sure that it ever had this influence on the church I served, but I did soon see this pattern of behavior by a few people in my ministry. A certain person once would not serve on the diaconate despite this person's displeasure with some things that were happening in worship and some decisions that were made by the church leadership, including the pastor (i.e. me!). This person initially had approached a member of the nominating committee to solicit a nomination to the diaconate. The goal, apparently, was to influence decisions in the future and even to question some decisions in the recent past. The goal was to make some changes. But this person would not serve on this committee because there were others who were already on the diaconate who were equally a source of displeasure, and these were people that I had nominated in previous years. So I guess in an indirect way this had an influence on the church and its ministries, because this person (in my opinion) should never have served there anyway. Situations like this were actually relatively rare, though. But this kind of thing did happen a few times.

When I was ill, I recalled and reflected on this conversation with a mentor in ministry, and I reflected on the frustration with life that sometimes led a person to seek out a place of influence within the church to make some changes and to set some things right. And I realized that, in many important ways, I was thinking and feeling what must have been the motivation for this church member who sought placement on a committee to help to get some things done in the church and to correct some obvious mistakes. Things were not as they should be, from a certain perspective, and service on a particular committee in a church provided an opportunity to help correct this. Things were certainly not as they should be in my life. And quite honestly if I had a say in the matter or a vote on the issue, things would be very different; they would be very different indeed! Cancer would never have been something that would have been a decision made by a committee on which I served.

I needed to admit a very strong urge in me. I very much wanted to serve on the committee that makes decisions on what happens in our fallen world. I was eager to get to work on this committee to set things right. In all honesty, I actually thought that I should be the chair of this committee. I wanted to be in charge of the important decisions for my life. Somehow, something had gone terribly wrong, and my guidance, counsel, and advice were needed on the direction of my life. What this really meant was that cancer was a huge mistake in the course of my life. Somehow, some way, God had let one slip through the cracks. I wanted to be God's counselor, to be his advisor in the very important matters that concerned me very much. To be God's advisor and to be his counselor—that is what I wanted!

I am merely expressing what I honestly thought and felt in this valley. Even though I knew better at the time, this is what I really wanted deep down in my soul. All of my theological training and experience in pastoral ministry, in lay ministry, and in the environment of Christian higher education prepared me for the proper and correct thing to think and say. I knew that only God is God. I knew that he does not need an advisor to help him run the universe. And I knew that I would not be a likely candidate for such a job, if one were open and available. But still, I really, really wanted to be on that committee!

Yet this is not my place, neither then nor now. Or ever. Only God is omnipotent and omnipresent. God alone is God, and he does not need my advice, perspective, or counsel: "Oh, the depth of the riches and wisdom and knowledge of God! How unsearchable are his judgments and how inscrutable his ways!" (Rom 11:33). God's wisdom and knowledge plumb depths that I cannot ever reach; humility is my proper place before God.[1] And praise is my proper response to God, who is sovereign over all things and who sustains all things.[2] The choices he makes for the progress of the kingdom of God follow paths that only he knows fully. Wright reflects well our proper place of humility before God:

> But this is the point in the argument [in Romans] when the only thing left to do is to take a long, deep breath and shake our heads in wonderment, and give praise to the God whose thoughts, plans and accomplishments are so much deeper and greater than anything we could have imagined for ourselves.[3]

When I come to him in prayer, it is not to advise him or inform him, but to petition him and to express my trust in him. I am a mortal human being who has a finite perspective on my own life, not to mention the course of the pathways of humanity and of the universe.

1. Moo, *Romans*, 391–92.

2. Barrett, *Commentary on the Epistle to the Romans*, 228.

3. Wright, *Paul for Everyone: Romans*, Part Two, 65.

No one is God's mental equal so that he or she may be God's counselor. God has no need for anyone to join him on the committee that runs the universe. No one may help God consider other options that are unknown or unseen to him: "For who has known the mind of the Lord, or who has been his counselor?" (Rom 11:34). The unexpressed answer to this question is quite obviously "No one!"[4] This quotation in Romans is from Isaiah 40, a passage that begins Isaiah's discourse on God's promise to restore Israel after the exile. This exile was God's punishment upon Israel for its repeated failure for many centuries to live faithfully within the covenant. Isaiah 40 is the beginning of an extended affirmation of God's promise to Israel, and this word of promise from God includes a call for comfort for God's people (Isa 40:1–2), the revelation of God's glory working on behalf of God's people (Isa 40:3–5), and a statement of the mortality of people and the brevity of their lives (Isa 40:6–8).[5] All of these are important themes that are developed elsewhere in Scripture in relation to suffering and which we also have explored in connection to this theme. God intends comfort and restoration for his people, and "it is a decision made solely by Yahweh. . . . Yahweh has planned *comfort* for the exiles, and none can prevent it."[6] God's plan and purpose are certain, despite recent events and current circumstances.

Isaiah's promise to Israel continues with an extended description of the uniqueness and the greatness of God (Isa 40:9–26). God is truly beyond compare and does not need advice or counsel. Israel, in the depths of the despair occasioned by the devastation of the exile, needed to hear a word from Isaiah about God, because their recent suffering might cause them to doubt this. They might doubt this both with respect to what was happening and with respect to God's intentions for their future. Had God forgotten his covenant with them? Had he forgotten them? This is the very question that Isaiah voices: "Why do you say, O Jacob, and speak, O Israel, 'My way is hidden from the Lord, and my right is disregarded by my God?'" (Isa 40:27). Everything in their recent experience indicated that God had forgotten them. Their covenant failure that God justly punished made it look as though this was the end of the road for Israel. God was done with them.[7] They were to be left in

4. Moo, *Romans*, 390.

5. Beyer, *Encountering the Book of Isaiah*, 164–65.

6. Brueggemann, *Isaiah 40–66*, 17.

7. Ibid., 27.

their suffering and misery. But Isaiah's word of promise indicated that this was not the case.

> Have you not known?
>   Have you not heard?
> The LORD is the everlasting God,
>   the Creator of the ends of the earth.
> He does not faint or grow weary;
>   his understanding is unsearchable.
> He gives power to the faint,
>   and to him who has no might he increases strength.
> Even youths shall faint and be weary,
>   and young men shall fall exhausted;
> but they who wait for the LORD
>   shall renew their strength;
> they shall mount up on wings like eagles;
>   they shall run and not be weary;
>   they shall walk and not faint. (Isa 40:28–31)

Even when God's people fail him and he must punish their failure to remain faithful to him, he speaks a word of comfort and promise to them. God is not finished with them, even when they suffer the devastation of the exile from the Promised Land. Only God is God, and only he knows the bright future promised to those who wait for the Lord to act on their behalf, despite recent events and current circumstances.[8] God's commitment to shepherd his people in all of life is never in doubt, even when circumstances seem to call into question God's love for his people, his knowledge of their troubles, and his plan for their future.

Paul's vision of God's greatness continues in Romans 11. It affirms that God is not obligated to return anything to anyone. He is the source of all things, he is the means for their accomplishment, and he is the goal toward which all things are aimed: "'Or who has given a gift to him that he might be repaid?' For from him and through him and to him are all things. To him be glory forever. Amen" (Rom. 11:35–36). As was the case with the previous question in verse 34, the unexpressed answer to this question also is, quite obviously, "No one!"[9]

> God is never in anyone's debt. It is a perpetual human failing to imagine that he is—to suppose that we can establish a claim on God either by our birth, our beauty, our brains or our behav-

---

8. Beyer, *Encountering the Book of Isaiah*, 167.

9. Moo, *Romans*, 390.

ior. But we can't. Nobody is ever in the position of giving God a gift which demands repayment while they sit back smugly, knowing they are in the right and waiting for God to get his act together.[10]

God owes no one a debt that he must repay nor does he owe anyone an explanation concerning his plan and purpose.

This description of God in Romans and Isaiah also reflects language elsewhere in Scripture, specifically in the Lord's final, climactic proclamation to Job in response to his question about God's intention and plan for his life: "Who has first given to me, that I should repay him? Whatever is under the whole heaven is mine" (Job 41:11). God speaks to Job and affirms that everything in creation is God's. No one can give to God so that he owes him anything, and he does not need a counselor nor is he indebted to anyone for anything.

Job's suffering is extreme, and his friends only compound his problem with their unfounded assertion that he is suffering for some specific and secret sin—and God is punishing him for this. Yet Job knows that this is not true and holds on to his integrity. Eventually he reaches a breaking point and seeks an audience with God. When God "shows up," it is neither to comfort nor to console him in his misery. It is instead to humble him.[11] Wilson notes that

> I have increasingly come to accept that there is simply no more effective way for the poet-author to depict a God who is so powerfully other than humans, who exceeds the bounds of complete human comprehension, whose ways are not our ways and whose thoughts are not our thoughts (Isa. 55:8–9), than to bombard Job with an overwhelming array of unanswerable questions that threaten to submerge him. This is not rebuke or even ridicule, but it is simply the author's attempt to demonstrate experientially what it is like for humans—even blameless and upright humans of great wisdom like Job—to enter into the presence of the sovereign God of the universe and of all time![12]

I sometimes hear Christians pray, talk, and sing about a desire for God to "show up" in some circumstance or situation, but I wonder whether or not we really understand the magnitude and significance of

---

10. Wright, *Paul for Everyone: Romans*, Part Two, 65–66.
11. Lawson, *Job*, 325–61; Alden, *Job*, 367–68; and Wilson, *Job*, 422–64.
12. Wilson, *Job*, 421.

what we are asking! God does "show up" in Job's life, and essentially he tells him to sit down and shut up—not to belittle or even to ridicule him but rather to establish most clearly and emphatically that he alone is God and to make perfectly clear that no one is qualified to assist or supervise him.[13] Job indeed responds in humility—only God is God and he does not need a counselor.[14]

I certainly knew this truth from Scripture. I had studied Romans both for a class in college and one in seminary. This passage from Scripture had long been a favorite part of Romans for me. A favorite Christian band had recorded a song that put this Scripture to music, and this song had often ministered to me throughout the ups and downs of life. I had often leaned on this vision of God in time of trouble in the past. I trusted its truth. Yet here I was in the middle of a battle with cancer, and I desperately wanted to change things. This could not be part of the plan. Something surely had gone wrong somewhere. God had let this one slip, or so it seemed to me. How could this be part of any plan with a good purpose? A mistake or oversight must have occurred, and I was the man for the job to get my life back on track. Indeed, I needed to help set things right—to change things back to where they should be for me and for my family.

Earlier in this book, I mentioned my friend Todd, whose music has been a great encouragement to me. He has another song that he began to write while his brother and his family endured suffering within their own family. Todd began to write this song, but it remained unfinished until he learned of my illness, when he began work on it again and completed it. I did not learn of this song and this story until a few years after my illness and I was finished with chemotherapy. We had the chance to visit with Todd, and he played this song for us in his living room. I have always enjoyed Todd's private concerts for us, and for obvious reasons this song is very special to me. It is essentially a prayer to God and is entitled, "You Are Good."

> You arrange the dark and painful seasons,
> As true as You declare the dawn of day.
> And though it's not for man to demand a reason,
> Sometimes, try as I may,
> I can't help but wonder why . . . why

---

13. Hafemann, *The God of Promise and the Life of Faith*, 157–60.

14. Lawson, 365–66; and Wilson, *Job*, 465–68.

But I know, I know
You have your reasons, though hidden from my eyes.
Yes, there is comfort in this one thing that I know,
I know, I know: You are wise.

You do as you please, Oh, what can man say?
None can stay your sovereign hand.
Your thoughts are not our thoughts;
Our ways are not your ways.
Let pain be precious to Your plan.
I need not wonder why . . . why

'Cause I know, I know
You have your reasons
No, I wouldn't change things even if I could.
'Cause You have a purpose in everything.
And I know, I know, I know: You are good.

And one day clouds of ancient mystery will break with joyful cries
As we look back on history through heaven's eyes,
Singing, "You are wise,"
Your ways are higher, as the heavens are above the earth.
Singing, "You are good."
Your thoughts are higher, as the heavens are above the earth.[15]

I love my brother, and I love his music, especially this song. And I affirm its truth, a truth that reflects Scripture. I am blessed by its profession of trust that God is good and wise as this song wrestles with the pain and suffering that is sometimes experienced in life. I am encouraged by its expression of Christian hope grounded in Christ's return. Yet I still hesitate to affirm in my heart and in my spirit one line from this song, despite the fact that I know it is true. It is this line from the chorus after the second verse: "No, I wouldn't change things even if I could." If I am really honest with myself, I actually would change this cancer if I could. I would go back and make it disappear; I would make it so that it had never happened. I would make things right.

I must confess that I wanted to be on the committee that runs the world so that I could correct and fix a huge wrong, namely, that I had cancer. This really could not be part of the plan. This made absolutely

15. MacDonald, "You Are Good." Todd's music is available at http://www.toddmac-donaldmusic.com.

no sense to me. Surely God had let this one slip through his watch. How could this be part of any divine plan? I wanted it then when I was in this valley, and I actually do want it now. If I could go back and change things, I would. There is not even the slightest doubt in my mind that I would do this, if I were able to do it. But I cannot, and I am not God. I don't have his knowledge or wisdom. I am a mortal human being whose knowledge and wisdom are fallible. My vision is limited by the horizons of my view, and even this I don't always see very clearly. Only God is creator of all things and the one who sustains all things. Only God is able to run the universe. I am not to be trusted with the running of the universe. I am not qualified for this job.

Moreover, I am not only a mortal, but I am also prone to be influenced by the things that God has created so that I am tempted to value them more than their creator. I often forget or ignore the truth that it is especially in pain that we are able to most clearly hear God. C. S. Lewis captures this poignantly: "God whispers to us in our pleasures, speaks to us in our conscience, but shouts to us in our pains: it is His megaphone to rouse a deaf world."[16] It is in the valley, when everything else is stripped away, that we see God for who he is, and we may grow to treasure him above all else. Lewis again puts it well, and he is worth quoting at length on this point:

> My own experience is something like this. I am progressing along the path of life in my ordinary contentedly fallen and godless condition, absorbed in a merry meeting with my friends for the morrow or a bit of work that tickles my vanity today, a holiday or a new book, when suddenly a stab of abdominal pain that threatens serious disease, or a headline in the newspapers that threatens us all with destruction, sends this whole pack of cards tumbling down. At first I am overwhelmed, and all my little happinesses look like broken toys. Then, slowly and reluctantly, bit by bit, I try to bring myself into the frame of mind that I should be in at all times. I remind myself that all these toys were never intended to possess my heart, that my true good is in another world and my only real treasure in Christ. And perhaps, by God's grace, I succeed, and for a day or two become a creature consciously dependent on God and drawing its strength from the right sources. But the moment the threat is withdrawn, my whole nature leaps back to the toys: I am even anxious, God forgive me, to banish

16. Lewis, *The Problem of Pain*, 93.

from my mind the only thing that supported me under the threat because it is now associated with the misery of those few days. Thus the terrible necessity of tribulation is only too clear. God has had me for but forty-eight hours and then only by dint of taking everything else from me. Let Him but sheathe that sword for a moment and I behave like a puppy when the hated bath is over—I shake myself as dry as I can and race off to reacquire my comfortable dirtiness, if not in the nearest manure heap, at least in the nearest flower bed. And that is why tribulations cannot cease until God either sees us remade or sees that our remaking is now hopeless.[17]

God sometimes uses our suffering to draw us to him. Sometimes he uses this pain to drive us there, even when we would not have chosen this path in life. This suffering still is not pleasant, and we may still sincerely and passionately wish for it to be gone or for it never to have happened. I see nothing in Scripture that encourages us to pretend that pain is pleasant or is even our own preference. But Scripture loudly proclaims that God, and God alone, is sovereign in all of life, even in and through suffering. It is especially in the valley of the shadow of death when everything else is stripped away that our need for God is laid bare and our longing for him intensified. As we walk with him in this valley, we can trust that his decisions do not need our advice or our counsel. And his decisions are both wise and good.

December 26, 2005

This will be a Christmas that I hope I never forget! All the kids are home, and it feels like heaven! God is doing what I knew he would do all along. He's healing Jeff. We received good news. That nasty chemo is working. The C.T. is normal, and the P.E.T. scan shows scar tissue—but, it's still in his bone marrow. That's the hardest area to clean up, apparently. There are still traces or residual signs of cancer in his marrow. So the oncologist has added another chemo drug. It's called Rituximub. It's biotherapy. This drug only attacks the cells that are cancer cells so it won't affect the red cell count or the white. The side effects for this drug are slight. But this needs to be administered in a very slow drip. We were there for 8 hours! This drug is given once a week for at least 1 month. That will mark the end of 6 months of treatment for cancer. Then I wonder if Jeff will have to have another bone marrow biopsy. But I'm just planning on Jeff going through this until the end of March.

17. Ibid., 106–7.

People continue to be of incredible help, especially financially! How on earth can we say thank you to everyone for all they have done?

A secret Santa came to the house and put gifts inside the door, including inner tubes for sledding. The tubes have a connection to people at the college, but I think the gifts are from my work, somehow. How can I say thank you when I don't know who it is?

I'm very thankful I don't have to go to work this week or run the kids anywhere! Or even go to Greek class. I need a break. A rest. I really need Christmas break this year. Next goal is spring break!

11

Can I Really Trust God? Or, the Breaking Point

Why, O Lord, do you stand far away?
Why do you hide yourself in times of trouble?
—Psalm 10:1

November 21, 2005
  At some point recently, I forgot how to pray. I was so numb, in shock, confused, and scared. I wanted to pray, but when I bowed my head and closed my eyes, I only cried. I was confused that I had suddenly forgotten how to pray! I didn't even know where to begin. But I rested in a Scripture that came back to me at that point. It was Romans 8:26–28.

November 21, 2005
  God, please heal my husband's sick body. I'm so used to him being in control—being strong and wise. And now he forgets so easily and can't think. I'm so selfish, I know, but I want to grow old with him. I don't want to be without him! I'm sorry, Lord, for my selfishness. We have so much life to live. He wants to see Sophia graduate and get married. These things I pray in your precious holy name. Amen.

I was not sure how much longer I could take it. The chemotherapy that I was receiving every two weeks was wearing me down with each new round of treatment. The side effects slowly began to take their toll on me. The chemotherapy for my cancer was four specific drugs: Bleomycin, Doxorubicin, Vinblastine, and Dacarbazine. Bleomycin is a particularly toxic drug, whose side effects include hair loss, weight loss, and nausea. After a few treatments, my oncologist noticed a slight wheeze in my breathing. Neither I nor my wife had noticed this, but he was on top of things, as usual. He ordered some tests for my lungs and determined that

Bleomycin was damaging them, as evidenced by scar tissue on my chest x-ray. After chemotherapy was over and this cancer was determined to be in remission, my doctor informed me that one in ten patients who receive Bleomycin die from the drug itself! Doxorubicin's side effects are too numerous to mention. Vinblastine is an especially nasty drug, trace amounts of which would pass through my system and be flushed from my body when I urinated. Its effects on young children are so aggressive that I was instructed to "double flush" the toilet after I urinated. An old farmer, who also received this drug and with whom I shared a treatment room, once told me of a time when he relieved himself out in the woods and watched as ants shriveled and smoked as he relieved himself on them! Vinblastin is so toxic that a nurse told me that if even a trace amount were to touch my skin or flesh, it would kill it. I asked this nurse the rather obvious question, to me at least: "Why doesn't it damage my veins, arteries, and heart?" The movement of my blood through them kept it from damaging these, she told me. Dacarbazine's side effects included loss of appetite, hair loss, and uncontrollable nausea and vomiting. Actually, I experienced all of the typical side effects from chemotherapy except nausea and vomiting. For whatever reason, I never threw up once. I came close a couple of times, but never once. I am grateful for this because I wondered about the impact on students of this side effect for me in the classroom when I was teaching!

The standard treatment for Hodgkin's Lymphoma was to receive this chemical cocktail (except for Bleomycin, which was removed from the mix after a few treatments) intravenously every two weeks for six to eight months. These four drugs have been the standard treatment for Hodgkin's Lymphoma for several decades. Despite the attempt of researchers to discover a better and more effective treatment, these remain the standard and fairly effective treatment for my disease. All four drugs needed to be given on a regular and fixed schedule. My doctor stressed this to me at the beginning. When four months were completed, my oncologist informed me that I would undergo tests, including a bone marrow biopsy, to see how much progress this chemo had made. After the first treatment in the middle of August, I thought that this would not be quite so bad after all. A bit of fatigue and a strange metallic taste in my mouth left me with little appetite. This was tolerable. My hair was not noticeably falling out either, despite the assurances from nurses to expect this. One of the drugs they nicknamed "The Cue Ball Drug!" But overall, this treatment for cancer would be something that I could endure.

My second scheduled treatment was like a warning shot across the bow. Blood work prior to chemo revealed that my white blood cell count had plummeted to a dangerously low level. It was well below the minimum that would allow me to receive treatment on that day. I sat on the exam table in shock and disbelief. I actually felt just fine, but I was not. And as I sat in that doctor's office, I recalled the oncologist's insistence that an every-fourteen-day cycle was the most effective treatment for this cancer. Any deviation from this would work against the chemotherapy's effectiveness.

I received an injection of Neupogen and was instructed to return the next day. My blood count then had rebounded nicely, and so I received my next chemo a day late. My oncologist told me that my body's reaction to Neupogen was a good sign because I would be able to resume this treatment. Without this drug to boost white blood cells in my body, I would not be able to continue with chemotherapy because the treatment itself would kill me long before the cancer. But I would need to have a series of injections for seven consecutive days in the middle of each two-week cycle. I could come into the doctor's office each day for this, but it would be more convenient for me, and presumably for them, if I took the shot at home. The prescription that he would write for me was for seven syringes that were prefilled with the proper dose of Neupogen. After each chemo treatment, he would renew this prescription. The doctor asked me a simple question. Could I give myself this shot at home? There was not a simple answer to this question, however. As someone who had lived most of his life in the passionate and intentional pursuit of the avoidance of needles into veins, there really was only one reasonable answer. I sat on the exam table for what must have seemed to be an eternity as I considered how I might form an intelligible response. I looked at Chris, to whom I had been married for twenty-four years and who knew me very well—well enough to interpret a mere glance. She immediately responded that she would give me the injections, if the doctor would show her how to do it. I have been and continue to be grateful for all that my wife has done and continues to do for me, but I honestly think that I have never been more grateful to her than I was at that moment.

The Neupogen was a great help to me, but it came with some side effects. The most significant, by far, was bone pain, which could be mild to moderate. Mine must have been more on the moderate end of the scale, at least. By the time that I received the final few injections during each cycle, the bone pain was persistent and would often come in waves, especially in my lower back. This pain was a sign that the drug was working as it stimulated new white blood cell production in my bone marrow, but it sometimes was difficult to bear. On a few occasions it was so severe that my hip bones hurt to the extent that they felt weak when I got out of bed and stood on my feet. Once my hips actually buckled, and I nearly fell down.

As the treatment cycle wore on, I began to feel the effects more and more. Fatigue, loss of appetite, muscle cramps, and a very weird pulsing sensation that would shoot down the muscles of my arms and legs were an increasingly constant companion. I became very sensitive to heat and to cold, and also to sunlight. In September, Chris and I traveled to the University of Minnesota to have a consultation with a specialist on Lymphomas. It was a very warm late September afternoon when we returned after this doctor's visit. A major accident on I–94 resulted in a traffic jam, which caused us to sit or creep along slowly for what seemed to be forever in a very warm car. I began to feel very ill, and I could not get comfortable. I wondered if I might actually die, because I had never felt this horrible in my entire life. It seemed to be the longest and last car ride of my life.

Ironically enough in all this, the day of chemotherapy was generally the best day of the two-week cycle. Despite sincerely expressed concern from lots of friends about the actual day of chemo, this was typically one of the better days for me in a cycle of treatment. The side effects would begin to bear down on me about twelve to twenty-four hours after treatment, and these would be persistent, and even intensify, for five to seven days. During the second week in a chemo cycle, the side effects would gradually begin to subside and my strength would slowly return. On the day of the next treatment, it had been two weeks since the chemicals had been pumped into me, and my body had recovered somewhat. I generally spent between three to five hours sitting in a reclining chair and hooked to an I.V. line. There was no place to go and lots of time on my hands. Throughout September and October, I had the chance to watch quite a few afternoon baseball games—not a bad day, indeed!

Despite the irony of my experience of the day I received chemotherapy, there was increasingly very little that was good about it. Every two weeks I coaxed myself back to the oncology clinic to sit in a chair. And coaxed is exactly the right word. By October, I felt that I had hit the bottom, physically and emotionally. By this third month of treatment, I regularly felt like I had had enough of this. It needed to stop, but it couldn't. The fatigue and the pain seemed to be endless and overwhelming. And I could not fight the thought that it all might be wasted effort. What if I went through all of this suffering and pain just to learn at the end that the cancer was still there? I knew that I needed to continue in this treatment, but, frankly, pessimism was difficult to resist. About two or three days before every treatment a pattern began to develop between Chris and me. At some point I would sit with her and confess my desire to stop treatment. Sometimes I would break down and weep at the prospect of more chemotherapy. I just could not do it. I was just starting to feel better and I didn't want to go back to the oncologist, but I did. Perhaps I just needed to say this, and Chris graciously allowed me to say it and listened to me. But, in reality, I really did want to stop, even though I knew what the likely end of this would be.

I have shared this experience of the devastating side effects of this chemotherapy with students in the classroom, and I have posed this question to them: What kind of moron goes back over and over again for this kind of treatment? Why would I continue to go back to this doctor when I knew that these next two weeks would be worse than those before it? I mean, the chemotherapy was far worse than the disease in terms of how I felt and how it impacted my body, at least up to this point. Prior to chemo, the symptoms of the cancer included a weird lump under my left arm, a bit of fatigue (but nothing like chemotherapy!), and night sweats that left me drenched from head to toe. It was only after I began treatment that I really began to feel "sick." What kind of a moron went back for this treatment? The kind who trusted the doctor's diagnosis—that this disease left unchecked would soon kill me—and the kind who trusted his plan for the treatment of my disease. Despite how it made me feel, this chemotherapy was intended to help me. I went back to the oncologist for treatment every two weeks because I trusted him. I trusted him even when everything that I was experiencing and feeling seemed to be killing me. I went back for this treatment because I trusted the oncologist's diagnosis and treatment plan, despite what I felt or how it was grinding me down and wearing me out.

November and December were very dark months for me, and frankly I don't remember much about them. This is probably a good thing. I did have a very serious sinus infection in November that required penicillin, and I needed a transfusion in December because I had become dangerously anemic. But perhaps the worst day of these two months was the day of the four-month test results. These tests would determine whether two more months or four more months of chemotherapy were needed in my treatment. When the oncologist shared the test results with us, I received the news with ambivalence and a bit of discouragement, frankly. Although these tests showed that there was significant progress in eliminating the cancer from my body, the results were still inconclusive. There probably was still cancer in my bone marrow, in particular. The growing pessimism in me pushed me toward despair. This treatment might, after all, prove ineffective in the end. At the very least, it seemed clear to me that I would need four more months of chemo, and I did not think I had this in me. I did not think I could do this anymore.

At some point during these two months I reached the point where I got down to some business with God. I had been a Christian since I was twelve years old. I had gone to college and seminary to prepare for service in Christian ministry. I had served in two churches and currently was serving in Christian higher education. I had trusted God and in his promises for most of my life, and I had trusted in his provision all along the way. I am not claiming that I was perfect, but simply that I was a Christian who was growing in his walk of faith. I had been one who professed trust and confidence in God for most of my life. But from the beginning of this battle with cancer, a primary struggle for me was the care of my family and the provision of their need. I had been a husband and father for a long time. Although we were never anywhere near anything like affluent, I always enjoyed the role of husband and father. Yes, I would have confessed that God is the giver of all good gifts and that I am dependent upon him. But, really, who would care for my family, if I died? Who would provide for them? At an abstract and theoretical level, of course, it was God; but at a deeply personal and emotional level, I was the answer to this question. I needed to be around for them.

I do not remember the date, but I remember the day well. It felt as though God was absent and might abandon me and my family in the time of our greatest need. Like the psalmist who expresses his pain in a lament, I cried out, "Why, O Lord, do you stand far away? Why do you hide yourself in times of trouble?" (Ps 10:1). Weak and pale from chemotherapy, I was thin and virtually hairless. I often remarked to Chris that I looked like Gollum! Physically, I was spent. Emotionally, I was drained. Spiritually, I was numb. Had God hidden himself from me in this suffering in the valley of the shadow of death?

Psalm 10 is a lament psalm that asserts the perspective of the wicked: that God is absent.[1] This psalm also implies that this perspective can influence the godly who suffer.

> Linking back to "times of trouble" mentioned in 9:9, Psalm 10 opens with agonizing questions directed to God, revealing a sense of isolation and divine absence that contrast with the confident affirmation of Yahweh as "refuge" in Psalm 9. Deliverance is not yet at hand in Psalm 10, and for the psalmist God seems hidden and removed (10:1).[2]

The wicked behave as they wish in order to satisfy their selfish desires, and they especially exploit the helpless (Ps 10:6–10). The danger is that of a predator who waits to pounce on unsuspecting prey or a hunter who sets a trap for his quarry.[3] This wicked behavior is motivated by the notion that God is removed from human experience and has hidden himself.

> For the wicked boasts of the desires of his soul,
>   and the one greedy for gain curses and renounces the Lord.
> In the pride of his face the wicked does not seek him;
>   all his thoughts are, "There is no God."
> His ways prosper at all times;
>   your judgments are on high, out of his sight;
>   as for all his foes, he puffs at them. . . .
> He says in his heart, "God has forgotten,
>   he has hidden his face, he will never see it." (Ps 10:3–5, 11)

The wicked person's arrogant assertion that there is no God is not really a statement of atheism, as we would understand this in our cul-

1. Goldingay, *Psalms*, 1:177–82; and Wilson, *Psalms*, 1:232–33.

2. Wilson, *Psalms*, 1:232.

3. Goldingay, *Psalms*, 1:181.

ture. The statement that there is no God is actually a denial of account-ability before God, as verse 11 makes clear.[4] In other words, "God is not involved in the everyday world."[5] The wicked think that there is no God who holds people accountable for their selfish and harmful behaviors. In his arrogance, the wicked person thinks that he is really the ultimate authority in his life and that he is the final arbiter of what is right and what is wrong in his life and in his conduct with others. And the opening questions of this psalm indicate that even the godly may be influenced by this perspective when they endure suffering. Is God hidden from the daily concerns of life? Is he absent when he is needed the most?

This was really my concern. Would God hide himself when I need-ed him the most? And for me the clear and compelling response from God to my illness and its potentially negative impact on my family was for God to heal me. This was something in which I could trust. This was my desire, and this desire in itself was fine. But what I wrestled with was how God would provide for my wife and my children if I died. I wanted God to continue to provide for them through me. Could I really trust God despite what I was experiencing and what I was feeling? Could I really trust God to provide for them if I were no longer here?

The lament psalms in Scripture regularly include a confession of trust in God and confidence in him, even in the midst of suffering. Psalm 10 is no exception.

> The LORD is king forever and ever;
>   the nations perish from his land.
> O LORD, you hear the desire of the afflicted;
>   you will strengthen their heart; you will incline your ear
> to do justice to the fatherless and the oppressed,
>   so that man who is of the earth may strike terror no more. (Ps 10:16–18)

Psalm 10 is a cry to the Lord to protect those who find themselves under the crushing weight of oppressors in this fallen world.[6] This psalm addresses the Lord as the eternal sovereign over all the earth.

> Yhwh's listening (v. 17a) is not just in the past. Yhwh continues to listen. . . . Yhwh habitually "bends an ear" to them, inclining

4. Wilson, *Psalms*, 1:233.

5. Goldingay, *Psalms*, 1:180.

6. Wilson, *Psalms*, 1:234–35.

> a head from the heavens so as to be able to hear exactly what is going on and to hear the cries that are being uttered down on earth. The result is indeed the kind of action that a king (cf. v. 16a) is committed to (v. 18). The king of a city is the one who has the power to do something about wrongdoing there, and the one who is morally obligated to do something about it.[7]

The Lord is sovereign over the earth, and he hears the cry of the afflicted, the fatherless, and the oppressed. All three of these were precisely the issue for me that day. I was afflicted and oppressed by this dreaded disease and the horrible effects of its treatment. More particularly, I was oppressed and afflicted by the prospects for my family. Would my children soon be fatherless? Would my wife soon be a widow?

My heartfelt and sincere desire was that this would not be the reality that my family faced, and I am confident that my desires for this were not necessarily wrong. There is nothing inherently wrong with the desire to live so that one may provide for his family. There is nothing wrong with the trust in God that he would provide for my family through my employment and my work. But the deeper question remained for me. Would I trust that God would provide for my family if I were no longer here? Could I trust God to provide for my family if I died? Could I actually say these words in a prayer of a profession of trust and confidence in him? It is one thing to affirm this in a statement of faith or to state it as one's confidence when the storms of life are nowhere in sight. It is another thing actually to pray these words to God.

Circumstances in life can conspire to call into question God's love for his children. Sometimes life's trauma assaults faith and trust in God's promises. Is God willing and able to deliver on his promises? Is perseverance in faith worth it? Perhaps God is willing—he loves deeply and wants the best for his children—but he lacks the ability to pull this off. Or perhaps he is able, but is unwilling for whatever reason. Suffering often allows thoughts like these to creep into our minds and our hearts.

It is precisely in these moments that we need to remember and to trust in God's demonstrated willingness and ability to deliver on his promises. God has already clearly demonstrated that he is on our side and that he has the willingness and the ability to keep his promises to us. This is not mere wishful thinking or a blind "leap of faith" theology. When we look at the cross and the resurrection of Jesus Christ, we see

---

7. Goldingay, *Psalms*, 1:184.

God's ultimate expression of his willingness and his ability to keep his promises.

> What then shall we say to these things? If God is for us, who can be against us? He who did not spare his own Son but gave him up for us all, how will he not also with him graciously give us all things? (Rom 8:31–32)

When we see the cross, we are seeing the ultimate expression of God's willingness to act on our behalf.[8] God did not spare his own beloved son but freely gave him for us. God willingly offered his own beloved son, and this demonstrates convincingly the extent of his commitment to his people. God did not spare the most beloved person to him; and if he has already done this, why would he fail to follow through on his promises? The cross of Christ thus has the capacity to destroy doubt that God is willing to act on our behalf. In the resurrection of Jesus Christ we see God's ability to keep his promises.

> Who shall bring any charge against God's elect? It is God who justifies. Who is to condemn? Christ Jesus is the one who died— more than that, who was raised—who is at the right hand of God, who indeed is interceding for us. (Rom 8:33–34)

The cross demonstrates God's willingness, and the resurrection demonstrates his ability to keep his promises despite the fearsome specter of Death.[9] Death itself cannot defeat God's plan and purpose. And it cannot separate us from the love of God in Christ Jesus (Rom 8:35–39). When circumstances conspire to call into question God's promises and his commitment to his people, Christian hope for the future is grounded on God's demonstrated willingness and ability to remain faithful to his people. The extent to which God is willing to go to keep his promises to us is demonstrated in the sacrifice of his beloved Son; the extent to which God is able to keep his promises is demonstrated in his power to raise Jesus from the dead.

I reached a day in the darkness of that December when I knew I needed to do this because, in fact, I really trusted more in me and not so much in him in this matter. I knew that I desperately needed to pray to God and to confess to him that I trusted him with my family, even if I were no longer here on this earth to provide for them. I needed to do

8. Moo, *Romans*, 282; and Wright, *Paul for Everyone: Romans*, Part One, 158–59.

9. Moo, *Romans*, 283; and Wright, *Paul for Everyone: Romans*, Part One, 159–10.

this for my own spiritual welfare because I had reached a breaking point in my walk with God. Could I trust my family to him? So, that day in the bathroom after a morning shower I collapsed onto the floor. Stripped of every pretense of self-sufficiency that this life can afford, I lay there and wept before God because I knew what I needed to say. But I was still very unsure if I could actually say the words. I knew I must very simply and directly, but most importantly verbally, profess to God that I trusted him to care for my family if I were no longer here on this earth to provide for them. I confessed that I really did not see how he could do so from my vantage point that morning, but I acknowledged that despite my ignorance and uncertainty, he was able to provide what they needed. I spoke this prayer to God out loud because I needed to do this. Once I had prayed this simple prayer, I did include my own desire to be here to be the one God used for this. I needed to be completely honest before God. In this prayer, I released my grip on what God's will looked like for my family, and in the middle of the valley I rested in God who is creator, sustainer, and provider. This remains the hardest prayer I have ever spoken out loud to God.

> *January 10, 2006*
> *It's hard to believe that we are now in the year 2006. I was begin-ning to wonder if this year would ever come for us! I pray this is a good year.*
>
> *On January 6th, we learned that he only has two more chemo treatments left. Then more testing. If the bone marrow is normal, well, I don't know if there is anything else. But if the cancer is still there, then we're facing a bone morrow transplant. This would be awful to go through. So far away. Isolation and living away from home.*

12

The Doctor's Statement . . .
and Only God Is Omniscient!

O LORD, you have searched me and known me!
You know when I sit down and when I rise up;
you discern my thoughts from afar.
You search out my path and my lying down
and are acquainted with all my ways.
—PSALM 139:1–3

February 3, 2006–A Kite Sighting
It's cold out today. Cold, but sunny and slightly breezy. Not spring-like at all. It's not April, yet. I saw the prettiest sight that made me think of spring. It reminded me of how God is. He's like spring. A fresh breath of air. Even on the darkest days.

I saw someone flying a kite on Lake Bemidji today. Not in a boat since it's February, and the lake is frozen solid. It's the dead of winter, everything on the ground is white, and the sky is gray. Winter can be so depressing.

There are seasons in our lives that can seem like winter. Cold and frozen in our walk with God. We're not growing, and we're wondering if God is even there. Even if the sky is blue, our hearts may be stuck in the dead gray sky of winter.

God melted my heart this winter. He allowed my husband to go through that horrid disease called cancer. Not that allowing my hubby to go through cancer is a good thing. But what we learned because of cancer is a wonderful thing. Even though we are in the middle of winter outside, my heart has been thoroughly warmed by God's unfailing presence in our lives. Like the warm sun on a fresh spring day. He has provided in ways I never expected, and He provided for us when I didn't know we needed to be provided for until the provision came. He has been in control of everything all along.

God has been there like that kite I saw today. Unexpected for this time of year. Even though I expect God to be there for all the seasons of our lives, sometimes we need to be taken by the shoulders, looked at straight in the eye, and reminded that God hasn't left us out in the cold.

What a sight to see that kite today on one of the coldest days of the year! And what a sight to see God at work in our lives during one of the most difficult seasons of our lives! This past six months with cancer in our home has been like a long, harsh winter. Yet, God has always been there. Like the sight of a kite soaring high in the middle of a long, cold winter.

To me, that kite was the promise of the spring that is yet to come. And God is bringing a new season into our lives as well. A season of good health. Today would have been a chemo day. But that treatment is over, for now. That yellow kite is a reminder. It's symbolic to me. I see a sign that promises a new coming season in our lives.

I remember the day well. I was sitting on an exam table in the doctor's office. It was a cold February day in northern Minnesota. It was the day when we learned that this cancer was in remission. Honestly, I thought that this day would never come. More accurately, I did not think that I had the strength to get to this point. The treatment for this cancer often seemed so harsh and so debilitating that I often wondered if it would claim me long before the cancer would.

Just a few weeks earlier I received my twelfth round of chemotherapy, which marked the end of six months of treatment. It was a great surprise, and even a shock, to hear from the oncologist in early January that this treatment would be my last in this particular chemotherapy. Prior to this announcement, he had given no indication my treatment would end at six months of chemo. The various tests that I had undergone in December after four months of treatment had shown good progress toward remission. There was no clear evidence of cancer in my lymphatic system or in my bone marrow. The results of the bone marrow biopsy were uncertain, though. No clear sign of cancer, but some ambiguous signs meant that it might still be lurking.

The chemotherapy for my Hodgkin's Lymphoma was six to eight months of treatment every two weeks, with tests at four months to determine the effectiveness of this treatment. I had taken these test results after four months and my oncologist's consultation on them to mean that I likely would need the full eight months of treatment. I really could not allow myself to think anything less than eight months, and the doctor gave me no indication at that time that I should expect anything less. I determined that I could not assume six months only to learn that I would need two more months of treatment beyond that time. This would have been devastating news for me, and I prepared myself for it with the expectation of the full eight months. But secretly I longed for only a few more treatments.

So it came as an unexpectedly pleasant surprise when the oncologist informed me that my twelfth treatment would be my last. He had decided that the progress indicated in my four-month tests in December was sufficiently good, and he thought it likely that these treatments over the last two months after these tests would be enough. He continued that in my case, given the progress indicated after four months of treatment, if six months of chemo had not been effective in putting this cancer into remission, another two months of treatment beyond this would not likely have any beneficial effect—certainly not enough to put me through the agony of another two months of chemotherapy. At the end of January and the beginning of February, he ordered the full range of tests to see if cancer remained. If these most recent test results did not show the cancer was in remission, other therapies would need to be considered. For some time, these had been lurking ominously on the horizon for me and my family. It was not clear at all what this meant. What could these tests and treatments involve? What would be their cost financially, emotionally, and physically? Only one thing was clear. The oncologist indicated that this next step in treatment would involve doctors and clinics that were four to six hours from Bemidji.

So after my last chemotherapy treatment in January, I underwent blood tests and another bone marrow biopsy. I also traveled to the Roger Maris Cancer Center in Fargo to have a Positron Emission Tomography scan, which is a type of nuclear medicine imaging that is able to detect very small traces of cancer in the body. Then I waited for the results. During this wait, my mind began to wander. What if cancer remained in my body? The oncologist had indicated that if this chemo proved to be ineffective in the end, then other treatments might help. But none of these were available to me at this clinic. I would need to travel to Minneapolis or beyond for these treatments. And a bone marrow transplant, which was a likely next step, would involve several months in a hospital away from home. What would happen next?

There I sat on the oncologist's exam table, waiting with Chris for his entrance and the news. When he arrived, he began the routine physical exam that I had before each treatment; he looked at the chart of physical data collected by the nurse, asked me the routine questions he always asked, and poked and prodded in the usual places. All the while, I waited anxiously for the news. My oncologist was always very thorough and careful in his treatment. And I am very grateful to him for this. But he surely recognized that this doctor's appointment was not routine because he moved through this exam more quickly than usual. And then he announced that the most recent tests showed no sign of the cancer in my body. He stated this news so briefly and directly that I was not quite sure what I had just heard. At first I was unsure if I had heard him correctly, so I looked at Chris to gauge her reaction. She was crying, but this actually did not help me very much right then!

So I repeated what I thought I heard him say to me—that all the tests showed no sign of cancer in me—and asked him to affirm that this was accurate. He repeated that all the tests indicated that there was no sign of Hodgkin's Lymphoma in my lymphatic system, in my blood stream, or in any of my vital organs. There was no evidence of this disease anywhere in my body. It was exactly the news that I had been hoping to hear and had been anticipating for months; yet it was, at that moment, almost too much to bear. I was stunned, surprised, and overjoyed all at one time!

Then the oncologist added a comment that made me smile. He stressed to me that he would not use the word *cured* for my condition, but rather he wanted to use the word *remission*. And he really emphasized this point to me. At first I did not really understand the reason for the distinction he wanted to make. But once he explained himself, I could not help but smile. He preferred to be this precise in his terminology, he said, because he could not be certain that the cancer was not actually there in my body. All he wanted to affirm was that the test results showed no sign or evidence of this cancer in me. It may still be there, but he just could not find it.

I sat there on that exam table in his office and could not help but smile. I hopped off, shook his hand, and thanked him sincerely for all that he had done for me. I was and am genuinely grateful to him for his diligence and his care in my treatment. He was an excellent doctor who was always on top of my condition. He gave me the best medical care anyone could expect or receive. But he was, in that moment, merely affirming his humanity and its limits. To the best of his ability to treat my cancer and to analyze my test results, he could see no cancer in me. And although I don't think he would put it quite this way, he was really saying that he was not omniscient. He was affirming in his own way that he was not God. Within the limits of human ability and knowledge, the cancer was gone. But he was not God, and thus was not omniscient. I appreciated his honesty and was grateful for the medical care that the entire staff at the oncology clinic had provided for me.

I only know one person who is omniscient. Scripture affirms that God is the one who knows everything, and he alone has this attribute.[1] Famously in Psalm 139, God knows us intimately and completely. He knows all of our ways: "O Lord, you have searched me and known me! You know when I sit down and when I rise up; you discern my thoughts from afar. You search out my path and my lying down and are acquainted with all my ways" (Ps 139:1–3). Only God is omniscient.[2] Scripture teaches this, and Christian theology throughout the ages has confessed it. Psalm 139 affirms that God can know everything about its author (Ps 139:7–15) and can even know his future (Ps 139:16–18).[3] God knows me and my circumstances wherever I go, and he even knows the future. God knows in advance all of our days and even the details of those days.[4] This is a knowledge that is beyond us, and even beyond our ability to comprehend it adequately or sufficiently. Our lives are in the hands of God who loves us and knows us better than we can imagine. In and through the

1. This basic point has been somewhat controversial in recent years with respect to knowledge of future events and choices. Although a full treatment of this controversy is well beyond the scope and intention of this book, I want to affirm my understanding that Scripture teaches that God knows the future, even the choices we make in life. This view of God's foreknowledge is generally affirmed (with some variety of emphasis and description about how God's foreknowledge and human choices relate to each other) across theological traditions and is reflected in works such as Hafemann, *The God of Promise and the Life of Faith*; Carson, *How Long, O Lord?*; Feinberg, *Deceived by God?*; and Olson, *Arminian Theology*. Recently a view called "Open Theism" has challenged this traditional view of foreknowledge, as reflected in Boyd, *Is God to Blame?* For reasons along the lines that Carson details (*How Long, O Lord?* 33–37, 199–246), I have not been persuaded to adopt this view of God's foreknowledge.

2. Lawson, *Psalms 76–150*, 333; Goldingay, *Psalms*, 3:629–31; and Anderson, *Psalms (73–150)*, 904–7.

3. Goldingay, *Psalms*, 3:640.

4. Lawson, *Psalms 76–150*, 334–35; Goldingay, *Psalms*, 3:635–36; and Anderson, *Psalms (73–150)*, 910.

dark experience of cancer, I had learned in new and fresh ways what it means to trust him through a very difficult valley. I was grateful for what the oncologist had done for me, but I trusted in God who knows exactly my condition and is my Shepherd in all of life, including the valley of the shadow of death.

A few years ago Chris made a quilt for me to remind us of God's faithfulness and mercy to us during my illness. This quilt has a yellow kite in the middle, surrounded by eight other red kites toward the edges of the quilt. It is a reminder of the experience that Chris had when she saw that yellow kite over Lake Bemidji. It is a reminder that God granted me remission from this cancer. God sustained us through a very dark valley in which we endured a time of trouble unlike anything we had previously experienced. God gave us strength and provided for us in many ways, and for this I am thankful to him. This ordeal with cancer seemed to consume us, and frankly there was little in the midst of it to encourage hope for remission. But he was merciful to me. He has allowed me to continue to live. I am enjoying the opportunity to see Brian, our oldest son, mature into a young man of strong character. I walked Meg, our oldest daughter, down the aisle on her wedding day. And I am thankful that God brought Joe, our son-in-law, into her life and into ours. I have watched our son, Tim, go to college to study music, and I have experienced the delight that comes when I attend a concert and hear the beautiful music of which he is a part in the Concordia Band and the Concordia Orchestra. I am thankful for these remaining few years with Jeffrey and Sophia before they go off to college and life. I eagerly anticipate what God has for them in college and in life beyond it, including another trip down the aisle with my daughter. I do not take these years and these experiences for granted. And God has granted me the delight of seeing my first grandson, Colton, who always makes me smile and who brings me great joy every time I see him. God has been merciful to me, and for this I am very thankful.

I wish that I had never written this book. More specifically, I wish that I had never gone through cancer, which provided the circumstance for the idea of this book. I wish that the occasion for this book's topic had simply never happened. But I did go through this horrible experience, and I learned some things about myself and about my need to grow to trust God through this valley. Prior to my illness I had often stressed to parishioners in the churches I served and students in the college classes I taught that the church desperately needs a biblical theology of suffering. Especially in the Western church where many of us are often insulated from suffering, we have a need to know what Scripture has to say about this important part of human experience in a fallen world.

This book attempts to make a contribution to this important need for the church, but it is certainly not the final word on this topic. It really only deals with one aspect of a biblical theology of suffering—the suffering that comes our way when an unexplained disease strikes. This study seeks to contribute to this topic, but the need for a fuller development of a biblical theology of suffering remains. For example, there are other reasons for our suffering in this world. Sometimes people suffer because they make poor choices in life, and other times people suffer because the poor choices of others collide into their otherwise peaceful lives. Consider the situation of a drunk driver who kills a young couple as they are driving home on a Friday night after a visit with friends. The resulting criminal conviction of the one and the deaths of a couple, along with the suffering endured by the family and friends of both are clearly a part of a fuller treatment of a biblical theology of suffering.[5]

But it is not part of this particular biblical-theological reflection on suffering. This book focuses on how Scripture informs and encourages us regarding one particular aspect of this topic, specifically, the suffering that comes to us due to disease and the prospect of death that we all face until the Lord's return. And this study also is intentionally refracted through a particularly nasty experience of suffering that was endured by me and by my family. This book is not an ivory-tower treatment of Scripture's teaching on suffering, nor is it a complete study of this topic. Instead, it is an intensely personal record of how Scripture prepared me for this time in a very dark valley and how it sustained me during suffering.

The need for reflection on suffering is important, even though it is not very pleasant. This need is great for several reasons. First, suffering often catches us off guard, but it is a regular part of this life in this age. This was an important focus of the first section of this book. Suffering

---

5. There are a number of books that address the problem of evil more broadly and the place of suffering within this theological problem. See for example, Carson, *How Long, O Lord?*; Wright, *Evil and the Justice of God*; Boyd, *Is God to Blame?*; Hauerwas, *Naming the Silences*; and Spencer and Spencer, *Joy through the Night*. These authors approach this topic from a variety of theological perspectives.

exists for people because of the fall. Humanity's rebellion introduced the pain, suffering, and death we experience into God's good creation. The problem of pain is one that humanity has made for itself. But God's plan to undo the damage done by humans involves the renewal of creation, a renewal that has begun now in the death and resurrection of Jesus Christ to inaugurate the kingdom of God and that will climax and culminate in the New Creation. Scripture comforts us with the affirmation that God is our shepherd who cares for us and provides for us, even in the valley of the shadow of death.

The need for a biblical theology of suffering for the church is significant because Scripture encourages us to recognize that suffering provides us with the privilege to share the love of Christ with those who are hurting and in pain. This theme was especially prominent in the second section of this book. I was greatly encouraged through my illness by the constant parade of cards and notes sent to me by family and friends. I know that many, many people prayed regularly for me all across the country, and even around the world. In fact, I know that people prayed for me from Britain to New Zealand. Chris, my wife, whose journal entries have enriched this book throughout, was a constant companion and encouragement to me. She often said to me during my illness that she wished she could take this cancer from me; she wished she had to bear the burden of this disease instead of me. And I know that she sincerely and genuinely meant this. But when she would say this, I would look her directly in the eyes and reply firmly that I would not give this to her, if I could. Never.

The third reason that I remain convinced that the church needs a biblical theology on this topic is because suffering provides us with compelling opportunities to grow in trust. In the midst of suffering, the believer is compelled to turn to God. This has really been a focus throughout this book, but it is especially prominent in the third section. When we face severe pain, grief, and suffering, we have little option because the alternative is even more painful to consider. Suffering removes any middle ground in our relationship with God, and Christians either grow to trust him more or seemingly turn from him.[6] We learn to trust God when everything else seems to be stripped away from us.

---

6. An example of the former is Feinberg, *Deceived by God? A Journey through Suffering*; an example of the latter is Ehrman, *God's Problem: How the Bible Fails to Answer Our Most Important Question—Why We Suffer*.

Chris's journal contains a poem that she wrote sometime toward the end of chemotherapy. She describes this poem in her journal: "I wrote this as I looked back and reflected on how we made it through this time. I spent so much time praying. Even when I didn't really remember how to pray, I think my soul communed with God every second of the day. And sometimes I'd listen to you sleep, and then I would know I could be alone in my fears."

While You're Sleeping

You've gone to bed. Your eyes are closed. I hear you breathing but I know you're not really resting while you're sleeping.

The house is quiet, the kids are motionless under their blankets. The cats asleep at their feet, while you're sleeping.

This should be the time when I shut my eyes and gain new strength to be at your side helping you through these trying days, while you're sleeping.

But while you're sleeping I crumble to my knees and some days I open my mouth to speak with God, and the words just won't come out.

While you're sleeping, I need to ask God to help you through this. To get to the next day. To keep you safe from all that worries me. I need to pray, but I just cry and rock to comfort myself because the words just won't come. While you're sleeping, I couldn't pray.

But, finally, one night while you're sleeping, when I wilt to the floor, the words gush from my mouth and between the sobs and rocks, I speak to God.

While you're sleeping, I ask God to help you bear the pain, to keep your feet steady, to make you strong again.

While you're sleeping, I pray for our children, that they will be okay when your hair falls out and that they'll be safe in their beds from their own fears.

While you're sleeping, I thank God for all the people he has recently brought into our lives. And for all the ways they help us, like praying for us when we can't pray for ourselves.

While you're sleeping, I ask God to give me strength to help you. I ask God to teach me to pray for you, and I cry now so you will not see me cry later.

On my knees, while you're sleeping, I cry for you. My heart is broken for you. And I finally understand the sickening feeling I have in my soul. I'm mourning for you. God cares for you and blesses my heart all while you're sleeping.

I have included this journal entry in my own work in this final chapter in order to acknowledge that she was indeed my partner through this very dark and very deep valley. In many important ways, I would never have made it through without her love, support, and encouragement. I am thankful to God each day for her. It somehow seems most appropriate at the end of this book to acknowledge this through the integration of one of her journal entries into my own work. She and I were in this together.

Prior to my illness, I thought that I could know why things happened in my life, if not now then in the future when I am in eternity. And I often heard other Christians say basically the same kind of things. I have grown to think that we may have confused our partial ability to see how God uses the pain and suffering we experience with the idea that we can know *why* in some exhaustive sense, especially when we are in heaven. In the future, we may see more clearly how God has used these horrible kinds of experiences for good in the lives of those who love him, although I am less certain of this now. I don't think that Scripture encourages us to assume that we will ever know why in any complete or exhaustive sense because we will never be God. We will always be creatures who need to depend on their creator. We are dependent upon God for life now as we walk with him in this life, even when we walk with him through the valley of the shadow of death. We will also be dependent upon our creator God when we walk with him in the New Heaven and the New Earth.

Bibliography

Alden, Robert. *Job*. The New American Commentary. Nashville: Broadman & Holman, 1993.

Alexander, T. Desmond. *From Eden to the New Jerusalem: An Introduction to Biblical Theology*. Grand Rapids: Kregel Publications, 2008.

Anderson, A. *Psalms*. The New Century Bible Commentary. Grand Rapids: Eerdmans, 1972.

Barrrett, C. K. *A Commentary on the Epistle to the Romans*. New York: Harper & Row, 1957.

Beyer, Bryan. *Encountering the Book of Isaiah: A Historical and Theological Survey*. Grand Rapids: Baker Academic, 2007.

Blomberg, Craig. *Matthew*. The New American Commentary. Nashville: Broadman, 1992.

Blomberg Craig, and Miriam Kamell. *James*. Exegetical Commentary on the New Testament. Grand Rapids: Zondervan, 2008.

Boyd, Gregory. *Is God to Blame? Beyond Pat Answers to the Problem of Suffering*. Downers Grove: InterVarsity Press, 2003.

Bruce, F. F. *The Gospel of John*. Grand Rapids: Eerdmans, 1983.

Brueggemann, Walter. *Deuteronomy*. Abingdon Old Testament Commentaries. Nashville: Abingdon, 2001.

———. *Isaiah 40-66*. Louisville: Westminster John Knox, 1998.

Carson, D. A. *How Long, O Lord? Reflections on Suffering and Evil*. Grand Rapids: Baker, 1990.

Edwards, Jonathan. "The Resolutions of Jonathan Edwards" [1722–1723]. Available on the web site The Writings of Jonathan Edwards, International Outreach, Inc. (last updated January 29, 2011. http://www.jonathan-edwards.org/Resolutions.html.

Ehrman, Bart. *God's Problem: How the Bible Fails to Answer Our Most Important Question—Why We Suffer*. New York: HarperOne, 2008.

Fee, Gordon. *Paul's Letter to the Philippians*. The New International Commentary on the New Testament. Grand Rapids: Eerdmans, 1995.

Fee, Gordon, and Douglas Stuart. *How to Read the Bible for All Its Worth*. Third edition. Grand Rapids: Zondervan, 2003 [1981, 1993].

Feinberg. *Deceived by God? A Journey through Suffering*. Wheaton: Crossway Books, 1997.

Gangel, Kenneth. *Joshua*. Holman Old Testament Commentary. Nashville: Holman Reference, 2002.

Goldingay, John. *Psalms*. 3 Volumes. Baker Commentary on the Old Testament Wisdom and Psalms. Grand Rapids: Baker Academic, 2006, 2007, 2008.

Guinness, Os. *Unspeakable: Facing Up to Evil in an Age of Genocide and Terror*. San Francisco: HarperCollins, 2005.

Hafemann, Scott. *The God of Promise and the Life of Faith: Understanding the Heart of the Bible*. Wheaton: Crossway Books, 2001.

———. *2 Corinthians*. The NIV Application Commentary. Grand Rapids: Zondervan, 2000.

Hagner, Donald. *Encountering the Book of Hebrews*. Grand Rapids: Baker Academic, 2002.

Hansen, G. Walter. *The Letter to the Philippians*. The Pillar New Testament Commentary. Grand Rapids: Eerdmans, 2009.

Hauerwas, Stanley. *Naming the Silences: God, Medicine, and the Problem of Suffering*. Grand Rapids: Eerdmans, 1990.

Hubbard, Robert. *Joshua*. The NIV Application Commentary. Grand Rapids: Zondervan, 2009.

Johnson, L. Timothy. *Hebrews*. The New Testament Library. Louisville: Westminster John Knox, 2006.

Keener, Craig. *Matthew*. The IVP New Testament Commentary Series. Downers Grove: InterVarsity Press, 1997.

———. *Revelation*. The NIV Application Commentary. Grand Rapids: Zondervan, 2000.

Lawson, Steven. *Job*. Holman Old Testament Commentary. Nashville: Holman Reference, 2004.

———. *Psalms 1–75*. Holman Old Testament Commentary. Nashville: Holman Reference, 2003.

———. *Psalms 76–150*. Holman Old Testament Commentary. Nashville: Holman Reference, 2006.

Lewis, C. S. *A Grief Observed*. New York: HarperCollins, 1994 [1961].

———. *The Problem of Pain: How Human Suffering Raises Almost Intolerable Intellectual Problems*. New York: Macmillan, 1962.

MacDonald, Todd. "The River Flows." *Walking* [CD]. Todd MacDonald, 2001. [Todd's music is available at http://www.toddmacdonaldmusic.com.]

———. "Storm." *Walking* [CD]. Todd MacDonald, 2001.

———. "You Are Good." *Pilgrims Here* [CD]. Todd MacDonald, 2009.

Marsden, George. *Jonathan Edwards: A Life*. New Haven: Yale University Press, 2003.

McConville, John, and Stephen Williams. *Joshua*. The Two Horizons Old Testament Commentary. Grand Rapids: Eerdmans, 2010.

McKnight, Scot. *The Letter of James*. The New International Commentary on the New Testament. Grand Rapids: Eerdmans, 2011.

Merrill, Eugene. *Deuteronomy*. The New American Commentary. Nashville: Broadman & Holman, 1994.

Moll, Rob. *The Art of Dying: Living Fully into the Life to Come*. Downers Grove: IVP Books, 2010.

Moo, Douglas. *2 Peter, Jude*. The NIV Application Commentary. Grand Rapids: Zondervan, 1996.

———. *The Letter of James*. The Pillar New Testament Commentary. Grand Rapids: Eerdmans, 2000.

———. *Romans*. The NIV Application Commentary. Grand Rapids: Zondervan, 2000.

Moore, Pam. *Life Lessons from the Hiding Place: Discovering the Heart of Corrie ten Boom*. Grand Rapids: Chosen Books, 2004.

Olson, Roger. *Arminian Theology: Myths and Realities*. Downers Grove: IVP Academic, 2006.

Piper, John. *God's Passion for His Glory: Living the Vision of Jonathan Edwards*; with the Complete Text of *The End for Which God Created the World*. Wheaton: Crossway Books, 1998.

Piper, John, and Justin Taylor. *A God-Entranced Vision of All Things: The Legacy of Jonathan Edwards*. Wheaton: Crossway Books, 2004.

Sailhamer, John. *Genesis Unbound: A Provocative New Look at the Creation Account*. Sisters, OR: Multnomah Press, 1996.

———. *The Pentateuch as Narrative: A Biblical-Theological Commentary*. Grand Rapids: Zondervan, 1992.

Scott, James. *2 Corinthians*. New International Biblical Commentary. Peabody, MA: Hendrickson, 1998.

Shyamalan, M. *The Village* [DVD]. Burbank, CA: Buena Vista Home Entertainment, 2005.

Spencer, Aída, and Bill Spencer. *Joy through the Night: Biblical Resources on Suffering*. Eugene: Wipf & Stock, 2007 [1994].

Terrien, Samuel. *The Elusive Presence: Toward a New Biblical Theology*. Eugene: Wipf & Stock, 2000 [1978].

Thielman, Frank. *Philippians*. The NIV Application Commentary. Grand Rapids: Zondervan, 1995.

von Rad, Gerhard. *Deuteronomy*. The Old Testament Library. Translated by Dorothea Barton. Philadelphia: Westminster Press, 1966.

———. *Genesis: A Commentary*. Translated by John Marks. Revised edition. The Old Testament Library. Philadelphia: Westminster Press, 1972.

Waltke, Bruce. *Genesis: A Commentary*. Grand Rapids: Zondervan, 2001.

Wilson, Gerald. *Job*. New International Biblical Commentary. Peabody, MA: Hendrickson, 2007.

———. *Psalms*. Volume 1. The NIV Application Commentary. Grand Rapids: Zondervan, 2002.

Wright, Tom. *Evil and the Justice of God*. Downers Grove: InterVarsity Press, 2006.

———. *Paul for Everyone: Romans*, Part One: *Chapters 1–8*, and Part Two: *Chapters 9–16*. Louisville: Westminster John Knox, 2004.

———. *Surprised by Hope: Rethinking Heaven, the Resurrection, and the Mission of the Church*. New York: HarperOne, 2008.